To: Sandy Kegan

Mallika

Buen Provecho

LA PUERTA AZUL COOKBOOK

DAILY FEAST

Chef Ramiro Jimenez

Photography by Colin Cooke

Cover and text design by Beth Farrell

Cover and text layout by Ethan Evanston

Photography by Colin Cooke

www.cookestudio.com

Photographs on pages 16, 24, 74, 106 by Ramiro Jimenez

Sea Script Company

Seattle, Washington

ISBN: 978-0-9785436-8-6

Library of Congress Card Catalogue No.: 2008932929

First Printing January 2009

Printed in Hong Kong

Sea Script

SEA SCRIPT COMPANY

www.seascriptcompany.com

206.748.0345

Mexican cuisine is very distinctive. Influenced by Spain, Mexico grows and cooks with many exotic ingredients, including a large variety of peppers used in the salsas and moles. After the Spaniards arrived in Mexico in the 16th century, they were followed by the Meztizos. The two cultures merged creating el Mestizaje which, over the centuries, developed into Mexico's unique cultural and culinary identity.

The History

In 1521 Spain invaded Mexico. Hernán Cortés Pizarro, was a Spanish conquistador who initiated the conquest of the Aztec Empire on behalf of Charles V, king of Castile and Holy Roman Emperor. Cortés was part of the generation of Spanish colonizers that began the first phase of the Spanish colonization of the Americas. He rode his army through Cozumel and Tabasco armed with heavy artillery, defeating the Mayas and continuing on to battle the Aztec Empire in search of the large treasure he had heard they possessed. Once the Spanish conquered Mexico, they stayed and ruled for almost 300 years.

Spanish rule came to an end in 1810 thanks to Miguel Hidalgo, a village priest and revolutionary leader who began the movement to fight for independence against Spain. With his famous shout "Viva Mexico!" and ringing la campaña de Dolores (Dolores's bell), Hidalgo helped put an end to hundreds of years of invasion and helped regain Mexico's freedom. Miguel Hidalgo is known as el Padre de la Independencia (the Father of Independence). We celebrate Mexico's Independence Day on September 16th.

Between 1910 and 1920, Mexico was immersed in the Mexican Revolution with leaders like Pancho Villa and la Division del Norte (the Division of the North), which was the name of his army of countrymen in the North of Mexico, and Emiliano Zapata who fought the battles in the south of Mexico. These two men were key players in the revolution against president and dictator Porfirio Diaz.

After the Mexican Revolution, when Mexicans were once again in control of Mexico, the country hosted three different groups of peoples—the natives, the descendents of the Spanish, and the mixed blood of the Spanish and the natives (Mestizos). This opened the door to a new era in Mexican culture, el Mestizaje. This blend of the native and Spanish cultures contributed to the fusion of foods as well as the way food is prepared in Mexico.

The Spaniards introduced new ingredients—rice, onion, garlic, and a variety of herbs and spices—as well as domestic animals including chicken, pork, and beef. The introduction of these ingredients helped to create a new style of cooking in which Spanish influence became prominent.

The two main staples in Mexican culture and cooking are corn and chiles. Mexican cuisine is also well enhanced by a large variety of fruits and vegetables, beans, chocolate, tomatos, calabaza, nopales, tomatillos, avocado, and epazote. These are some of the ingredients used in tortillas, gorditas, quesadillas, ensaladas, sopas, salsas, adobos, and moles.

Mexico City, the capital of Mexico, is where foods and ingredients from throughout the regions are featured. You can walk down the street and have a feast sampling all kinds of antojitos (finger food).

You can stroll through el Mercado de la Merced o Central de Abastos (the city's market) and see a variety of peppers, herbs, moles, and vegetables that inspire you to try new dishes. El Mercado is where the central, south, and north regions of Mexico congregate to display the richness of their heritage and traditions and to proudly showcase their foods.

Basics in Mexican Cooking

Maiz

Corn is a cereal grain that was domesticated in Mesoamerica and spread to the other continents and the rest of the world after the Spanish came to America in the 16th century.

One of the basic ingredients in Mexican culture and cooking, corn was discovered by Quetzalcoatl, one the many Aztec gods. Quetzalcoatl comes from the Nahuatl language that millions of people still speak in Mexico today. The name Quetzalcoatl is derived from quetzal (colorful bird from Mesoamerica) and coatl (serpent) and means la Serpiente Emplumada (the plumed serpent).

Corn is used on a daily basis in Mexico, primarily in tortillas, which are served at lunch and dinner. Corn is also cooked in many Mexican dishes such as antojitos, especially in regions in central and southern Mexico, Puebla, Morelos, and Oaxaca from where most of the antojitos come. Tostadas, enchiladas, and picadas are among the many dishes that feature corn.

Chiles

Chiles, or peppers, are the other main ingredient in Mexican cuisine. People are sometimes intimidated by the use of chiles without realizing there are a variety of chiles with different flavors, aromas, and scales of spiciness from the mild to the very hot. Interpretation of spiciness varies from one person to another—what is mild for one person may be too hot for another.

Peppers can be eaten raw, cooked, dried, stuffed, or powdered. Their most common use is in salsas and moles to add color, aroma, and flavor.

Mole or mulli (Nahuatl) is the name for sauces whose primary ingredient is chile or a combination of chiles. Thanks to regions like Oaxaca and Puebla, Mexican cuisine is known around the world for foods and moles made with chiles.

TABLE OF CONTENTS

Complementos

Salsas

Postres

Bebidas

Glossary

La Puerta Azul Cookbook represents a chapter in my life that began a few years ago. While growing up with my family in Mexico City, I was exposed to good traditional flavors every day at home. My mother would cook flavorful meals as well as teach us what to do with the leftovers. We would see how quickly mole de pollo from the evening meal could be turned into enchiladas de pollo for lunch the next day. She showed us that, with Mexican cooking, creativity is always present—every sauce can be served with three or four dishes and leftover chicken or steak can easily become a delicious meal of tacos, tostadas, quesadillas, or enchiladas.

Our family often traveled to other regions, such as Oaxaca, Guerrero, and Puebla, visiting friends and family and experiencing new dishes. We would go to el Mercado (the street market) to eat and taste the differences and similarities of the food amongst the regions. We would learn new ways of preparing meals with new ingredients, flavors, and textures. I was always impressed with the pride the local people took in their cooking. I learned that preparing a meal is more than just the food, it's our shared culture, tradition, and identity. This passion for Mexican food and culture is what we had in common and from this, comes my motivation and inspiration.

Unlike even a decade ago, today we are able to get fresh ingredients from Mexico at local markets in most cities in the United States—a variety of peppers, tortillas, vegetables, and herbs. When it comes to traditional Mexican cooking, it's not just using the right ingredients or the way we present the food on a plate that makes for a delicious meal, it's also the steps we take preparing our ingredients and the techniques we employ to cook a dish that helps maintain the consistency of great food every time.

This cookbook is an opportunity to share with you the authentic traditional flavors of Mexico with an upscale touch. It moves beyond the stereotype and shows that Mexican cuisine is more than spicy food, tortillas, peppers, and rice and beans as many people still think of Mexican cooking. The recipes presented are a taste of the Mexican culture incorporating not only the passion and dedication for Mexican food that we enjoy at La Puerta Azul, but also the Mexican traditions and the colorful décor that infuses the restaurant.

The purpose of *La Puerta Azul Cookbook* is to share with you the best ingredients and techniques to prepare and enjoy the best Mexican dishes, including a variety of peppers and herbs to enhance your soups and sauces, without making them too spicy.

Cooking is a lifelong journey for me—everywhere I go and with every person I talk to, I learn new things that inspire me more and more to share my Mexican heritage and our delicious food with you.

—Chef Ramiro Jimenez

¡BIENVENIDOS!

LA PUERTA AZUL RESTAURANT

2510 Route 44

Salt Point, NY 12578

(845) 677-AZUL (2985)

www.lapuertaazul.com

GRACIAS

To everyone who helped me develop *La Puerta Azul Cookbook* and who, with their knowledge, inspiration and contribution, have made this book possible, my deepest gratitude—

Brad and Ash Reifler, for giving me the trust and the privilege of working at La Puerta Azul with the opportunity to accomplish my professional goals.

My mother Felipa Justo and my father Aristeo Jimenez, who inspired me at a very young age with their recipes and their home cooking, which I enjoyed throughout my childhood.

My wife Jan and my daughters Gabrielle and Kyra, for their unconditional love, support, and willingness to share their time with the restaurant business.

My sous chef Cassandra Cotoia, for her contagious energy and passion for food.

Douglas Rodriguez, my friend and mentor, who opened the doors for me in this business and has always been an inspiration to me.

Danny Kowel, talented pastry chef, who worked with me at my previous restaurant developing recipes and ideas.

All my friends for investing their time with me, and all those who shared their knowledge and traditions in all the cities and towns I visited in Mexico, I appreciate all of you.

And to Beth Farrell and Sea Script Company for the help and contribution they provided toward making this book a reality.

APERITIVOS

APPETIZERS

Ceviche Verde de Salmon

Ceviche de Atun

Bocoles Veracruzanos

Setas al Ajillo

Picadas

Tacos de Bistec a la Parilla

Tacos de Pollo

Tostados de Tinga

Tostados de Cangrejo

Ceviche

Ceviche is a blend of fresh fish or seafood that is partially cooked with citrus juices, such as lemons or limes. The seafood can also be blanched, which means it is cooked before making the ceviche. This method is popular for seafood like shrimp, mussels, clams, lobster, and calamari.

Ceviche is popular in regions near the Gulf of Mexico or the Atlantic Ocean including Acapulco, Veracruz, Oaxaca, and Chiapas.

In Mexico, all seafood is cooked prior to making ceviche and before mixing it with other ingredients. Another good way to prepare ceviche is by combining the freshest ingredients available and preparing the ceviche a la minute.

I like to quickly marinate the fish in lemon or lime juice and blend the other flavors with it so that the integrity of the fish's flavor is not lost.

Ceviche will always be only as good as the ingredients used to make it. The freshness of the ingredients is as important as the final product.

Picadas

Picadas or sopes are small corn masa cakes with pinched edges to hold the fillings. They're a great appetizer when you get together with friends or family. It's fun when everyone helps make the picadas.

Picadas are one of the dishes we used to make with my mother on Sundays. The whole family would enjoy an early dinner, making picadas with a variety of salsas and toppings such as chorizo, chicken, or beef.

CEVICHE VERDE DE SALMON

SALMON CEVICHE

SERVES 4

- 1 lb tomatillos
- 1 jalapeño pepper, stem and seeds removed, roughly chopped
- ½ cup orange juice
- 1 cup cilantro, loosely packed
- 1 lb salmon filet, skin and blood line removed
- 3 limes
- 1 red tomato, diced small (about 1 cup)
- ½ bunch scallions or green onions, washed, diced small
- Salt to taste

Garnishes:
- ½ cup cilantro leaves
- 3 red Mexican radishes, sliced julienne
- ½ red onion, cut in half, then quartered, thinly sliced julienne
- 1 cup Jalapeños Curtidos (page 64)
- Sliced avocado
- Tortilla chips

Peel and wash the tomatillos. Dry with paper towels. In a blender, purée the tomatillos, jalapeño, orange juice, and cilantro until smooth. Season with salt.

Dice the salmon and place in a bowl. Season with salt and the juice of 1 lime. Add the tomatoes, scallions, and additional lime juice, if desired.

Divide the salmon mixture into 4 individual serving bowls. Pour the tomatillo purée over each portion. Mix gently and season to taste. Garnish with cilantro leaves, radishes, red onion, Jalapeños Curtidos, and sliced avocado.

Serve with tortilla chips.

CEVICHE DE ATUN

TUNA CEVICHE WITH BASIL

SERVES 4

- 1 lb fresh tuna
- 1 bunch scallions or green onion, chopped
- 1 cup diced tomato
- 2 oranges, peeled, separated into segments
- ¼ cup fresh lime juice
- Salt to taste
- 2 cups Basil Purée (page 26)
- 1 small red onion, cut in half, thinly sliced
- 1 cup cilantro leaves
- 1 cup Jalapeños Curtidos (page 64)

Cut the tuna in small dices and place in a mixing bowl. Add the scallions, tomato, and orange segments. Add the fresh lime juice. Season with salt and gently mix well.

Place the ceviche in individual bowls. Add a drizzle of Basil Purée. Garnish with red onion, cilantro leaves, and Jalapeños Curtidos.

BOCOLES VERACRUZANOS
SMALL CORN POCKETS

MAKES 8 BOCOLES

- 3 cups maseca
- 2 tsp salt
- 1 tsp baking powder
- ½ cup melted lard or vegetable oil
- 1½ to 2 cups warm water
- 1 cup vegetable oil for frying

Fillings:
- 2 cups Frijoles Refritos (page 69)
- 2 cups Tinga de Pollo (page 39)
- 1 lb Carne a la Parilla (page 72)
- 2 cups Salsa Cruda (page 84)
- 2 cups queso cotija

In the bowl of a stand mixer using the dough hook, thoroughly combine the maseca, salt, and baking powder. Add the lard. Continue to mix on low speed until the mixture starts to look crumbly. Scrape the sides of the bowl with a rubber spatula to ensure the lard is evenly distributed. Add the water to the dough, ½ cup at a time (you might not need all of the water), until a soft dough forms. Scrape the sides of the bowl while mixing. You will know the dough is the right consistency when you squeeze a small portion into a ball and it holds together without being crumbly or breaking around the edges. Wrap the dough in plastic wrap and let rest for 1 hour.

Divide the dough into 8 equal balls, about 4 ounces each.

Preheat the comal or griddle over medium heat.

Preheat the oil in a pan to 350°.

Using a tortilla press and 2 pieces of plastic wrap (a 1-quart freezer ziplock bag split open works best), gently press each ball to make ½" thick gorditas that are 5" in diameter.

One at a time, place a gordita on the comal. Cook for 2 to 3 minutes or until each side is golden brown. Carefully transfer the gordita to the pan of hot oil. Fry on each side for 20 seconds. Remove from the oil and drain on paper towels.

Make a 2" to 3" cut in the thin edge of the gordita to make a pocket. Stuff the gordita with Frijoles Refritos, Carne a la Parilla, Salsa Cruda, queso cotija, or your favorite filling.

SETAS AL AJILLO
SAUTÉED MUSHROOMS

MAKES 4 CUPS

- ½ cup olive oil
- 3 tbsp chopped garlic (7 to 8 cloves)
- 4 pasilla chiles, stems and seeds removed, cut in half
- 2 lbs cremini mushrooms, sliced (about 12 cups)
- ¼ cup chopped parsley
- Salt and freshly ground black pepper to taste

In a very large sauté pan over medium high heat, add the oil, garlic, and pasilla chiles. Stir occasionally for 2 to 3 minutes.

Add the mushrooms to the pan and cook 15 to 20 minutes until a deep brown color, stirring occasionally. Season with salt and pepper to taste.

Transfer the mushrooms to a bowl and sprinkle with parsley.

PICADAS
SAVORY CORN CAKES

MAKES 14 PICADAS

- 3 cups maseca
- 2 tsp salt
- ¼ cup melted lard or vegetable oil
- 2½ cups water

Fillings:
- 3 cups Frijoles Refritos (page 69)
- 2 cups Salsa Cruda (page 84)
- 2 cups diced white onion
- 3 cups queso cotija

In the bowl of a stand mixer using the dough hook, thoroughly combine the maseca and salt. Add the lard. Continue to mix on low speed until the mixture starts to look crumbly. Scrape the sides of the bowl with a rubber spatula to ensure the lard is evenly distributed. Add the water to the bowl, ½ cup at a time (you might not need all of the water), until a soft dough forms. Scrape the sides of the bowl while mixing. You will know the dough is the right consistency when you squeeze a small portion into a ball and it holds together without being crumbly or breaking around the edges. Wrap the dough in plastic wrap and let rest for 30 minutes.

Divide the dough into 8 equal balls, about 4 ounces each.

Preheat the comal, griddle, or heavy skillet over medium heat.

Using a tortilla press and 2 pieces of plastic wrap (a 1-quart freezer ziplock bag split open works best), gently press each ball into a 4" in diameter.

Brush the preheated comal with oil or lard. One at a time, place the picada on the comal and cook until each side is light golden brown, about 2 minutes per side. Remove from the griddle and let cool slightly. When cool enough to handle, gently pinch up the edges of the picada to form a little wall around the edge. Place the picada back on the comal, flat side down. Cook 1 to 2 minutes until the bottom is crispy.

To serve, spread the picadas with Frijoles Refritos and top with Salsa Cruda, diced onion, and cheese.

You can also add toppings like Tinga de Pollo (page 39), grilled steak, Mexican chorizo, or roast chicken and have a feast with friends and family.

Tacos

When we think about Mexican food, the first thing that comes to mind are tacos. Tacos are one of the most festive and popular dishes in Mexican cuisine and in Mexican culture in general. Tacos can be eaten as a snack or a full meal.

Taco is also an expression used when a person is hungry or needs to eat quickly, "Me voy a comer un taco." "I'm going to grab a quick bite."

A taco is a warm, soft tortilla filled with any edible ingredients, folded in half, and garnished with onion, cilantro, and a squeeze of fresh lime juice.

Tacos are great for a reunion with friends. Have a table ready with tortillas, garnishes, guacamole, different salsas, and a variety of fillings. Let the party start by having your friends and family make their own tacos.

People enjoy tacos because they are quick, delicious, and simple to make. They can be made with whatever you choose—beef, chicken, pork, potatoes, or vegetables. You can even make tacos with *recalentados* (reheated leftovers).

Tostadas

Tostada refers to a crispy flat corn tortilla shell served with different toppings and garnished with lettuce, cheese, and salsa.

Tostadas are usually served as an appetizer and are easy to prepare. They are Mexican *antojitos* that can be prepared with a variety of toppings such as chicken, beef, pork, or even dry stews like tinga de pollo.

Some tostadas are served with a layer of puréed black beans, not only for flavor, but also to help the filling stick to the tortilla, preventing it from falling off.

Traveling to Puebla so many times, I fell in love with tostadas de tinga, my favorite. The flavor of the chicken and the texture of the tortillas are amazing.

TACOS DE BISTEC A LA PARILLA

GRILLED STEAK TACOS

SERVES 4

- 2 lbs Carne a la Parilla (page 72)
- Salt and freshly ground black pepper
- 12 Tortillas de Maiz (page 62)

Garnishes:
- 2 cups Rajas de Poblano (page 65)
- 2 cups Tomatillo Salsa (page 81)
- 2 cups Salsa Roja (page 77)
- 1 cup diced white onion
- 1 cup chopped cilantro
- 2 limes, cut in wedges

Preheat the grill to medium high.

Season the marinated steak with salt and black pepper. Grill to the desired temperature. For medium rare or medium, grill for 4 to 5 minutes on each side. Remove the steak, cover, and let rest.

Reheat the tortillas on a hot comal or griddle for a few seconds on each side. Transfer the tortillas to a cloth-lined basket to keep moist.

Slice the steak into thin strips against the grain and serve on a platter. Serve with the garnishes.

Note: 2 pounds of skirt steak makes about 4 cups, grilled and sliced. For an appetizer-size taco, fill each tortilla with ¼ cup of steak. For an entrée-size taco, fill each tortilla with ½ cup of steak.

TACOS DE POLLO
CHICKEN TACOS

SERVES 4

- 2 lbs Pollo Adobado (page 73)
- 12 fresh Tortillas de Maiz (page 62)
- 2 cups Chile de Arbol Salsa (page 79)
- 2 cups diced white onions
- 1 cup Rajas de Poblano (page 65)
- 1 cup chopped cilantro
- 4 limes, cut into wedges

Preheat the grill to medium high.

Season the chicken with salt and pepper. Grill the chicken, turning over every 4 to 5 minutes, until they are cooked through.

(One of the best and safest ways to cook chicken is to mark your chicken on the grill first and finish cooking it by baking it in the oven at 475° for 5 to 10 minutes or until cooked through.)

Slice the grilled chicken into thin strips and serve on a platter. Set out the basket of warm tortillas and festive bowls filled with salsa, onions, rajas, cilantro, and lime wedges to fill and garnish the tacos.

Note: 2 pounds of grilled chicken makes about 4 cups. For an appetizer-size taco, fill each tortilla with ¼ cup of chicken. For an entrée-size taco, fill each tortilla with ½ cup of chicken.

TOSTADAS DE TINGA
CHICKEN STEW TOSTADAS

SERVES 4

- 2 cups Frijoles Refritos (page 69)
- 2 cups Tinga de Pollo (page 39)
- 8 tostada shells (corn tortillas fried flat into a flat crisp)
- 2 cups queso fresco
- 2 cups Salsa Cruda (page 84)
- 1 small red onion, cut in half, thinly sliced julienne
- 2 avocados, peeled, pit removed, cut in wedges
- Jalapeños Curtidos (page 64)
- 1 small head iceberg lettuce, sliced julienne

Reheat the Frijoles Refritos and Tinga de Pollo and let simmer for 3 to 5 minutes to heat through. Set aside.

Spread ¼ cup of the Frijoles Refritos gently (to avoid breaking) on each tortilla. Add ¼ cup Tinga de Pollo and cheese. Top the tostadas with Salsa Cruda, onion, avocado, jalapeños, and lettuce.

TOSTADAS DE CANGREJO

CRAB TOSTADAS

SERVES 4

- 1 lb crabmeat
- ½ cup mayonnaise
- 1 red tomato, diced (about 1 cup)
- 1 cup Jalapeños Curtidos (page 64)
- ½ cup diced red onion
- ¼ cup chopped cilantro
- 4 limes
- 1 small jicama, peeled, thinly sliced julienne (1 cup)
- 1 mango, peeled, sliced julienne (about 1 cup)
- 8 tostada shells (corn tortillas fried flat into a flat crisp)
- 1 cup cilantro leaves for garnish
- Salt and freshly ground black pepper to taste
- 2 cups Salsa Roja (page 77)

Clean the crabmeat, making sure there are no shells, and place in a medium bowl. Add the mayonnaise, tomato, ½ cup of the chopped Jalapeño Curtidos, onion, cilantro, and the juice of 2 limes. Season with salt and black pepper. Stir gently to avoid breaking up the crabmeat too much.

In a small bowl, combine the jicama and mango with the juice of ½ lime. Adjust the seasoning with salt and black pepper. Add more lime juice if desired.

Gently spread the crabmeat mixture onto each tostada shell. Garnish with the jicama-mango mixture, jalapeños, and cilantro leaves.

Serve on a platter with Salsa Roja.

SOPAS

SOUPS

SOPA DE FRIJOL

BLACK BEAN SOUP

SERVES 4

- 12 cups water
- 2 cups black beans (14 oz), picked clean of debris, rinsed
- 1 bay leaf
- 1 tbsp dried oregano
- 2 epazote sprigs
- 3 tbsp vegetable oil
- ½ white onion, diced (about 1 cup)
- 2 tbsp chopped garlic (7 to 8 cloves)
- 2 tsp ground cumin
- Salt and freshly ground black pepper to taste

Garnishes:
- Crema fresca
- Sliced avocado

In a medium stockpot over medium high heat, combine the water, beans, bay leaf, oregano, and epazote. Bring to a boil. Reduce the heat and simmer uncovered.

In a small sauté pan, heat the oil over medium heat. Add the onion and garlic. Cook for 5 to 7 minutes or until the onions are translucent. Add the cumin into the onion mixture, stirring constantly to toast the cumin, about 1 to 2 minutes.

Add the sautéed onion mixture to the simmering pot of beans. Season with salt and pepper. Continue to simmer uncovered over low heat for 4 hours or until the beans are tender and creamy in the center. Add boiling water to the stockpot, if needed, so that the beans are always covered by at least 1" of water to cook evenly. Remove the beans from the heat and let cool for at least 10 minutes.

Purée the beans with a stick blender or in batches in an electric blender. Reheat before serving. If the soup is too thick, add more water until it is the desired texture.

Ladle into individual serving bowls. Garnish with crema fresca and sliced avocado.

CALDO DE POLLO
CHICKEN BROTH

MAKES 12 CUPS

- 2 lbs bone-in chicken
- 12 cups cold water
- 1 medium onion, peeled, chopped
- 1 medium carrot, peeled, chopped
- 4 garlic cloves, cut in half
- 2 celery ribs, chopped
- 2 bay leaves
- 1 bunch cilantro stems (reserve leaves for other recipes or garnishes)

Combine all the ingredients in a medium stockpot over medium high heat. Bring to a boil. Reduce the heat and simmer for 1 hour or until the chicken is cooked and a flavorful broth has developed.

Strain the broth to use immediately or cool it down and refrigerate for up to 3 days. Broth can be frozen in smaller batches. Reserve the cooked chicken for another use.

SOPA DE MAIZ
CORN SOUP

SERVES 4

- 1 poblano pepper
- ¼ lb unsalted butter (1 stick)
- 1 large white Spanish onion, chopped (about 2½ cups)
- 4 cups corn kernels (about 6 ears of corn)
- 4 cups Caldo de Pollo (page 19)
- 1 cup heavy cream
- 2 tbsp granulated sugar
- 1 cup mushrooms, thinly sliced, sautéed for garnish
- 4 cilantro sprigs for garnish
- Salt to taste

Roast the poblano pepper on an open flame or on the grill until the skin is blistered. Remove the pepper from the grill and place in a small bowl. Cover with plastic wrap to steam. When the pepper has cooled, peel off the skin and stem, remove the seeds, and roughly chop. Set aside.

In a small stockpot over medium heat, melt the butter. Add the chopped onions and sauté, stirring constantly for 5 to 7 minutes or until the onions are translucent. Stir in the corn and sauté for another 5 minutes.

Pour the Caldo de Pollo into the corn mixture and bring to a boil. Reduce to a simmer. Add the reserved poblano pepper and the cream, stirring to thoroughly combine. Simmer for an additional 15 minutes. Remove the soup from the heat and let cool for at least 15 minutes.

Working in batches, purée all the ingredients in a blender until the soup is almost smooth (there should still be some texture). Return the soup to the stockpot and bring to a simmer. Add the sugar and season with salt. Mix well.

Ladle the soup into individual serving bowls. Garnish with sautéed mushrooms and cilantro.

Note: For a vegetarian corn soup, replace the chicken broth with vegetable stock.

SOPA DE CALABAZA
ROASTED PUMPKIN SOUP

SERVES 4

- 1 3-lb pumpkin, peeled, cut into 1" cubes (about 10 cups)
- 1 large Spanish onion, diced (about 2½ cups)
- 1 oz ginger, peeled, diced
- 3 cloves garlic, peeled
- 1 tsp salt
- ¼ cup vegetable oil
- 4 to 6 cups Caldo de Pollo (page 19)
- 1 cup heavy cream
- ½ tsp ground nutmeg
- Roasted pepitas (pumpkin seeds) for garnish
- Salt to taste

Preheat the oven to 350°.

On a baking sheet, toss together the pumpkin, onion, ginger, garlic, salt, and oil. Spread the vegetables out on the baking sheet. Bake in the oven until tender when pierced with a fork, about 30 minutes.

In a medium stockpot, bring 4 cups of Caldo de Pollo to a simmer. Add the roasted vegetables and simmer for 25 minutes. Purée the soup in batches in a blender. Thin the mixture with additional Caldo de Pollo, if needed, to make a nice creamy texture.

Add the puréed soup back to the stockpot. Stir in the cream and nutmeg. Bring back to a gentle simmer just to warm through. Season with salt. Stir for 1 minute and remove from the heat.

Reheat the soup before serving. Garnish with toasted pepitas.

Note: This soup may be made up to 2 days in advance or frozen, but do not add the cream, nutmeg, and salt until just before serving.

SOPA DE TORTILLA

TORTILLA SOUP

SERVES 4

- 2 tbsp vegetable oil
- 1 white onion, diced (about 1 cup)
- 2 garlic cloves, peeled, chopped
- 3 red beefsteak tomatoes, diced (about 3 cups)
- 6 cups Caldo de Pollo (page 19)
- 2 epazote sprigs
- Salt to taste

Garnishes:
- 1½ cups cooked chicken, shredded
- 1 cup queso fresco
- 3 corn tortillas, cut in strips, fried until crisp
- 3 guajillo chiles, cut in strips
- 1 avocado, peeled, pit removed, cut in wedges
- 4 cilantro sprigs
- 2 limes, cut in wedges

In a stockpot over medium heat, add oil, onion, garlic, and tomatoes. Sauté 8 to 10 minutes or until the onions are translucent.

Transfer the vegetables to a blender and purée until smooth. Return the puréed vegetables to the stockpot. Bring to a gentle simmer. Cook for 2 minutes, stirring constantly.

Add the Caldo de Pollo and epazote. Bring to a boil. Reduce the heat and simmer for 10 minutes. Season with salt.

Serve the soup garnished with chicken, queso fresco, tortilla strips, guajillo strips, avocado, and cilantro. Squeeze a wedge of lime juice over the top of each serving.

ENSALADAS

ENSALADA DE TOMATE

TOMATO SALAD

SERVES 4

- 5 beefsteak tomatoes, cut in small chunks
- 2 avocados, cut in small chunks
- 1 cup green olives, sliced
- 1 chayote, sliced julienne
- 2 limes, juiced
- 2 cups Basil Purée (recipe below)
- Salt and pepper to taste
- 2 cups crispy tortilla strips
- Mache leaves for garnish

Basil Purée (makes 2 cups):
- 8 cups water
- 4 cups basil leaves
- 1½ cups vegetable oil
- Salt to taste

For the Basil Purée:
In a medium size pan, bring the water to a boil. Add basil and cook for 10 seconds. Quickly transfer to an ice bath to cool off. Drain the water. Using paper towels, pat the basil dry.

Chop the basil and transfer to a blender. Add the oil and purée for 3 minutes or until the purée is bright green. Season with salt.

For the salad:
Mix the tomatoes, avocados, olives, and chayote in a large mixing bowl. Add lime juice and the basil purée. Season with salt and pepper.

Serve on individual plates, making sure you have enough of each ingredient on each of the plates. Add more basil purée, if needed. Garnish with tortilla strips and mache.

ENSALADA DE NOPALES

CACTUS PAD SALAD

SERVES 6

- 2 lbs nopales (cactus pads)
- 2 red tomatoes, diced small
- 1 small white onion, diced small
- 1 tbsp chopped fresh oregano
- ¼ cup olive oil
- 3 limes
- 5 red radishes, shaved
- 1 cup queso fresco, crumbled
- 1 tbsp chopped cilantro
- Salt to taste

In a large pot, bring the water to a boil. Season with salt and the juice of 1 lime. (This will help reduce the sliminess of the cactus.)

Peel the cactus pads, making sure all the needles are removed. Place the pads in the boiling water and simmer for 20 minutes. Drain the water and set aside to cool.

Dice the cooled cactus pads. Mix them in a bowl with the tomatoes and onions. Add the oregano, oil, and the juice of 2 limes. Season with salt.

Serve the salad garnished with the radishes, cheese, and cilantro.

ENSALADE DE CALABAZITAS CON ADEREZO DE MIEL

ZUCCHINI SALAD WITH HONEY VINAIGRETTE

SERVES 4
MAKES 2 CUPS VINAIGRETTE

- ½ cup honey
- ¼ cup balsamic vinegar
- 2 tbsp Dijon mustard
- 1 cup olive oil
- 2 bunches watercress, washed and dried
- 1 small red onion, cut in half, thinly sliced (about 1 cup)
- 1 cup pumpkin seeds, toasted
- 1 chayote, sliced julienne
- 3 zucchini, cut in ¼" circles, grilled
- 2 red tomatoes, cut in half, thinly sliced (about 1 lb)
- 2 cups crumbled goat cheese
- Salt and freshly ground black pepper to taste

For the honey vinaigrette:
In a medium size mixing bowl, whisk together the honey, vinegar, and mustard. Slowly add the oil, whisking constantly until the mixture is thoroughly mixed and creamy. Add salt and black pepper. Set aside.

For the salad:
In a large mixing bowl, add the watercress, onion, pumpkin seeds, and chayote. Gently toss with the honey vinaigrette. Season with salt and black pepper.

Arrange the zucchini and tomatoes alternately in a circle around the perimeter of 4 salad plates. Place salad in the center of each plate. Garnish with crumbled goat cheese.

ENSALADA DE EJOTES

GREEN BEAN SALAD

SERVES 4

- 2 tbsp olive oil
- 1 tbsp chopped garlic (about 3 cloves)
- 1 small white onion, diced medium (about 1 cup)
- 1 red tomato, diced medium (about 1 cup)
- 1 lime, juiced
- 2 lbs green beans, stems removed, blanched
- Salt and freshly ground black pepper to taste

In a medium size sauté pan over medium heat, add the oil and garlic. Sauté until the garlic is a light golden brown, about 5 minutes. Add the onion and tomato. Cook 5 to 7 minutes or until the onion is translucent, stirring often. Season with lime juice, salt, and black pepper. Stir well.

Drizzle the sauce over the beans.

This salad can also be served as a side dish to accompany Pollo a Limon (page 58), Salmon con Calabaza (page 48), or Pescado a la Veracruzana (page 47).

ENSALADA DE TORTILLA

TORTILLA SALAD

SERVES 4

Vinaigrette:
- ½ cup peanuts, toasted
- ½ cup orange juice
- ¼ cup red wine vinegar
- 2 chiles de arbol, stems removed, toasted
- 1 cup olive oil
- Salt and freshly ground black pepper to taste

Salad:
- 2 cups green beans, blanched, cut in half
- 2 red tomatoes, diced (about 1 cup)
- 1 small red onion, diced (about 1 cup)
- 1 head romaine lettuce, chopped
- Salt and freshly ground black pepper to taste

Garnishes:
- 1 cup queso cotija
- 2 avocados, cut in wedges
- 6 corn tortillas, cut in strips, fried until crisp

For the vinaigrette:
In a blender, add the peanuts, orange juice, vinegar, and chiles de arbol. Process until almost smooth. With the blender on slow, slowly add the oil until the vinaigrette is very smooth. Season with salt and pepper.

For the salad:
In a large salad bowl, combine the green beans, tomato, onions, and romaine lettuce. Season with salt and black pepper.

Lightly dress the salad with vinaigrette. Sprinkle with cotija cheese. Top the salad with avacado and tortilla strips. Add additional vinaigrette, if needed.

ENSALADA DE LA CASA

HOUSE SALAD
SPINACH SALAD WITH APPLES AND MUSTARD VINAIGRETTE

SERVES 4

Vinaigrette:
- ½ cup Dijon mustard
- ½ cup orange juice
- ¼ cup red wine vinegar
- 1 cup vegetable oil
- Salt and freshly ground black pepper to taste

Salad:
- 2 cups baby spinach
- 2 cups watercress
- 1 cup romaine lettuce, chopped
- 2 granny smith apples, cut in wedges
- 1 tomato, diced (about 1 cup)

If you cut the apples in advance, keep then in a small container with a splash of orange juice to prevent then from turning brown.

In a medium size mixing bowl, whisk together the mustard, orange juice, and vinegar. Whisking continuously, slowly add the oil until the vinaigrette is a thick, creamy consistency. Season with salt and black pepper.

In a large bowl, toss together the spinach, watercress, and romaine. Add the vinaigrette and salt and pepper to taste. Arrange the apples in a circle around the perimeter of each salad plate. Place the greens in the center of the plate. Sprinkle the tomatoes on top of the salad. Add more vinaigrette, if necessary.

ENTRADAS

ENTRÉES

Quesadilla de Hongos

Quesadilla de Pollo

Enchiladas de Pollo

Tinga de Pollo

Chile Relleno

Barbacoa de Pollo

Costilla en Adobo

Caldo Michi

Pescado a la Veracruzana

Salmon con Calabaza

Camarones al Pastor

Mixiote de Borrego

Filete y Papas con Rajas

Costillas con Ejotes

Pollo al Limon

Lomo de Cerdo

Quesadillas

Quesadillas, like most Mexican antojitos, are street food or finger food and very simple to make. You can make quesadillas with anything you want, leaving an open door to your imagination and creativity.

Quesadillas are normally cooked on a comal which gives a nice golden brown color to the tortilla and a slightly crisp texture to the outside. A griddle or non-stick pan also works well.

To prepare quesadillas, all you need are fresh corn or flour tortillas, cheese, and any fillings you want to add—chicken, beef, mushrooms, or grilled vegetables. Your fillings should be fully cooked with the exception of the fresh herbs.

Oaxaca and Chihuahua cheeses are traditionally used when you make quesadillas.

Enchiladas

Enchilada is Spanish for "in chile sauce." Enchiladas are a traditional Mexican dish made with corn tortillas quickly dipped in hot oil or lard to soften the tortilla. They can be filled with almost anything—chicken, beef, vegetables, or cheese. The tortillas can be either rolled or folded in half after adding the filling.

The filling should be fully cooked and seasoned before assembling the enchiladas. The enchiladas are baked in a casserole in the oven and topped off with Salsa Roja or Salsa Verde and garnished with onions, cheese, and crema fresca.

Enchilada Sauce should be prepared in advance before assembling the enchiladas.

QUESADILLA DE HONGOS

MUSHROOM QUESADILLA

SERVES 4

- 8 6" corn or flour tortillas
- 2 tbsp vegetable oil
- 2 cups Oaxaca cheese
- 2 cup sliced mushrooms or Setas al Ajillo (page 7)
- 2 cups Rajas de Poblano (page 65)
- 4 sprigs epazote, chopped
- Salsa Roja (page 77)
- Guacamole de la Casa (page 70)

Preheat a comal, cast-iron griddle, or heavy skillet over medium heat.

Brush one side of a tortilla with oil and place on the hot comal. Spread ¼ cup of cheese on the tortilla, leaving a small border around the edge. Add the mushrooms, Rajas de Poblano, and epazote. Top with another tortilla. Gently press the top of the quesadilla down with the back of a spatula. Heat until the bottom of the tortilla develops light brown spots.

Lightly brush the top of the tortilla with oil. Flip the quesadilla to toast the other side and to finish melting the cheese. Remove from the heat.

On a cutting board, cut the toasted quesadilla into quarters. Repeat the process with all of the tortillas.

Serve with Salsa Roja and guacamole.

QUESADILLA DE POLLO

CHICKEN QUESADILLA

SERVES 4

- 8 6" corn or flour tortillas
- 2 tbsp vegetable oil
- 2 cups Oaxaca or Chihuahua cheese
- 2 cups Pollo Adobado (page 73), cut in strips
- 1 cup Jalapeños Curtidos (page 64)
- 2 cups Tomatillo Salsa (page 81)
- Crema fresca

Preheat a comal, cast-iron griddle, or heavy skillet over medium heat.

Brush one side of a tortilla with oil and place on the hot comal. Spread ¼ cup of cheese on the tortilla leaving a small border around the edge. Add the Pollo Adobado and Jalapeños Curtidos. Top with another tortilla. Gently press the top of the quesadilla down with the back of a spatula. Heat until the bottom of the tortilla develops light brown spots.

Lightly brush the top of the tortilla with oil. Flip the quesadilla to toast the other side and to finish melting the cheese. Remove from the heat.

On a cutting board, cut the toasted quesadilla into quarters. Repeat the process with all of the tortillas.

Serve with Tomatillo Salsa and crema fresca.

ENCHILADAS DE POLLO

CHICKEN ENCHILADAS

SERVES 4

- 6 cups Salsa Rojo para Enchiladas (page 85) or Salsa Verde (page 86)
- 2 cups vegetable oil
- 2 tbsp chopped garlic
- ½ cup diced onion
- 1 cup chopped red tomato
- 4 cups shredded chicken (page 39)
- ¼ cup chicken stock
- 12 6" corn tortillas (home made or store bought)
- Salt and pepper to taste

Garnishes:
- 2 cups queso fresco
- 1 cup chopped white onion
- 2 cups crema fresca

Preheat the oven to 375°.

In a medium size pan, bring the Salsa Rojo para Enchiladas or Salsa Verde to a low simmer.

Heat 3 tablespoons of oil in a large pan over medium heat. Add the garlic, onion, and tomato. Sauté until the onion is translucent. Stir in the shredded chicken. Let simmer until hot. Add chicken stock as needed to keep the chicken moist. Season with salt and pepper. Remove from the heat and set aside to cool.

In a medium size pan, heat the oil to 350°. One at a time, dip the tortillas into the oil for 5 seconds. Remove and place on paper towels.

Fill the tortillas with ¼ cup of the chicken mixture. Roll or fold the tortillas.

Place the stuffed tortillas on a platter large enough to hold all the tortillas. Pour the enchalada sauce over the tortillas so that the tortillas and platter are covered. Cover the platter with aluminum foil. Bake in the oven for 10 minutes.

Using a spatula, place 3 enchiladas on each plate. Garnish with cheese, onion, and crema fresca.

TINGA DE POLLO

SPICY CHICKEN STEW

MAKES 6 CUPS

- 2 lbs boneless chicken breasts
- 4 garlic cloves, crushed
- 8 sprigs fresh thyme
- 2 bay leaves
- 3 chipotle peppers
- 2 tbsp vegetable oil
- 2 white onions, sliced in slivers (about 2½ cups)
- 1 tbsp minced garlic (about 3 to 4 cloves)
- 3 red tomatoes, diced (about 3 cups)
- 1 tsp ground cumin
- Salt and freshly ground black pepper to taste

For shredded chicken:

In a stockpot over medium high heat, bring the chicken breasts, garlic cloves, 2 thyme sprigs, and bay leaves to a simmer. Cook for 20 to 30 minutes or until the chicken is cooked through. Remove the chicken from the broth and let cool. Reserve the chicken broth.

Shred the chicken into small pieces, making sure there are no skin or bones.

In a food processor, purée the chipotle peppers with ½ cup of the reserved chicken stock. Set aside.

Remove the leaves from the remaining thyme sprigs.

In a medium pan over medium heat, add the oil, onion, and garlic. Cook 5 to 7 minutes until the onions are translucent, stirring occasionally. Add the tomatoes, thyme leaves, cumin, and chipotle mixture. Bring to a simmer. Add the shredded chicken. Add more chicken broth if necessary to make a slightly soupy mixture.

Season with salt and black pepper to taste. Simmer for about 10 minutes before serving. This mixture should be moist but not too soupy.

CHILE RELLENO
STUFFED PEPPERS

SERVES 6

- 6 medium poblano peppers
- 3 potatoes, peeled, diced small (about 3 cups)
- 2 tbsp vegetable oil
- 2 tomatoes, diced (about 2 cups)
- 1 white onion, diced (about 1 cup)
- 1 tbsp chopped garlic (about 3 cloves)
- 4 cups Oaxaca cheese
- 3 cups Sopa de Frijol (page 18)
- Guacamole de la Casa (page 70)
- Crema fresca
- Salt and freshly ground black pepper to taste

Preheat the oven to 375°.

Roast the poblano peppers on the grill or over the open flame of the stove until blistered. Place the peppers in a bowl and cover with plastic wrap. Let cool.

When the peppers are cool enough to handle, peel off the skins, leaving the stems on. Make a small cut into the side of each pepper to remove the seeds. Set aside.

Place the potatoes in a small saucepan. Cover with water. Salt the water and bring to a boil. Reduce to a simmer. Cook the potatoes until they are fork tender. Do not overcook. Remove the pan from the heat and drain.

In a small pan, heat the vegetable oil, tomatoes, onion, and garlic. Cook until the onion is translucent. Set aside to cool.

In a bowl, mix together the potatoes, tomato mixture, and the cheese. Season with salt and pepper.

Carefully stuff the peppers with the filling. Set the filled peppers on a baking sheet. Bake for 10 minutes or until the cheese is melted.

Serve the chile rellenos in individual bowls with ½ cup of Sopa de Frijol. Top with Guacamole de la Casa and crema fresca.

BARBACOA DE POLLO
STEAMED CHICKEN

SERVES 6

- 12 chile guajillos, stems and seeds removed
- 1 tsp ground cumin
- 3 garlic cloves
- 2 bay leaves
- 2 avocado leaves
- 1 cup orange juice
- 6 chicken breasts, skin on
- Banana leaves
- 1 white onion, sliced thin (about 1 cup)
- Salt and freshly ground black pepper to taste

This is a dish that is best prepared in the morning to be cooked for dinner.

In a medium sauté pan over medium heat, toast the guajillo chiles for about 2 minutes or until the chiles start to release their aroma. Remove from the heat. Set aside to cool.

In the same pan over medium heat, toast the cumin, garlic cloves, bay leaves, and avocado leaves for about 2 minutes, stirring frequently. Be careful not to burn them.

In a food processor or blender, add the orange juice, chiles, and toasted spices. Purée until well blended and the chile pods are broken into small pieces.

Season the chicken with salt and pepper. Place in a non-reactive pan or a ziplock bag. Add the puréed chile mixture. Let marinate for 4 or 5 hours in the refrigerator.

Set up a steamer basket over a simmering pot of water.

Cut the banana leaves into 6 squares, about 10" x 10". Place 1 chicken breast on each of the banana leaves. Discard the remaining marinade. Top each of the 6 pieces of chicken with the sliced onions, dividing equally.

Gently wrap the banana leaf snugly around each piece of chicken making 6 bundles. Wrap each bundle snugly with plastic wrap to ensure they don't open while cooking, and to reserve the juices of the meat and the marinade.

Place the bundles in the steamer. Cover and steam for 20 minutes or until the chicken is cooked. The easiest way to check the doneness of the chicken is to insert a meat thermometer into the center of one of the bundles.

Barbacoa de Pollo can be prepared with chicken thighs or legs if you prefer dark meat. If using dark meat, cook for 25 minutes.

COSTILLA EN ADOBO

BRAISED PORK RIBS

SERVES 4

- 2 racks baby back ribs
- ½ cup vegetable oil
- 4 mulato chiles
- 4 ancho chiles
- 4 pasilla chiles
- ½ cup sesame seeds
- 2 tbsp sliced almonds
- 6 cloves
- 1 cinnamon stick
- 2 tbsp raisins
- 8 cups water
- 1 white onion, diced small (about 1 cup)
- 6 garlic cloves
- 1 tbsp dried oregano
- ¼ cup raisins
- Salt and freshly ground black pepper to taste

Preheat the oven to 450°.

Cut each rib rack into 4 sections. Wash the ribs in cold running water and dry with a paper towel. Season with salt and pepper.

In a hot skillet, heat the oil over medium high heat. Sear the ribs on the meat side for 4 to 6 minutes or until golden brown.

In a medium sauté pan over medium heat, toast the mulato, ancho, and pasilla chiles for 2 minutes or until the chiles start to release their aroma. Remove from the heat. Set aside to cool.

In the same sauté pan, toast the sesame seeds, almonds, cloves, and cinnamon stick for 2 to 3 minutes, stirring constantly, until they release their aroma. Be careful not to burn them. Remove from the pan. Set aside to cool.

Bring 4 cups of water to a boil. Reduce to a simmer and add the toasted chiles, onion, garlic, oregano, and cinnamon. Add more water, if needed, to ensure everything is covered. Simmer for 10 minutes. Set aside to cool.

In a food processor, purée the simmered ingredients. Add the raisins, roasted almonds, sesame seeds, and cloves to make the adobo. The mixture should be thin enough to easily baste the ribs.

(*continued on next page*)

Set the ribs in a large roasting pan. Pour the adobo over the ribs, making sure the ribs are covered with liquid. Add more water, if needed. Cover the pan with foil. Cook the ribs in the oven for 1 hour or until the meat is tender. Reduce the leftover liquid to use as a sauce for the cooked ribs.

Serve the ribs on individual plates with a generous portion of Arroz Rojo (page 67) and Ensalada de Nopales (page 28).

CALDO MICHI
MAHI IN SPICY TOMATO BROTH

SERVES 4

- 5 red tomatoes, cut into wedges (about 5 cups)
- 1 white onion, diced large (about 1½ cups)
- 4 garlic cloves
- 2 cups water
- 3 chayotes, diced in 1" cubes
- 1 lb white cabbage, thinly sliced (about 5 cups)
- 4 chile morita, stems and seeds removed, toasted
- 3 tbsp vegetable oil
- 4 8-oz mahi mahi filets
- 2 epazote sprigs
- 2 fresh thyme sprigs
- 1 lime
- Salt and freshly ground black pepper to taste

Preheat the oven to 425°.

Line a baking sheet with aluminum foil. Spread the tomatoes, onions, and garlic in an even layer on the sheet. Roast for 30 minutes.

Blanch the chayote in a large of pan of salted water for 5 minutes. Remove from the pan. Spread out on another baking sheet to cool. Using the same water, blanche the cabbage for 2 minutes. Set aside to cool.

In a medium sauté pan over medium heat, toast the chiles for 2 minutes or until they start to release their aroma. Remove from the heat. Set aside to cool.

In a blender, purée the roasted vegetables and chiles. Set aside.

Season the fish on both sides with salt and pepper.

Heat the oil in a large sauté pan over medium heat. When hot, sear the fish on one side for 2 minutes. Turn the fish over. Sear for 2 more minutes. Remove the fish from the pan

Using the same pan, add the puréed vegetable/chile mixture. Bring to a simmer. Add the water cabbage and the chayotes. Bring back to a simmer. Add the epazote and thyme sprigs. Bring back to a simmer. Simmer for 5 more minutes. Add the fish back into the pan and cover. Simmer for 4 more minutes or until cooked through, making sure the fish does not break.

Serve the fish in a bowl over a generous portion of Arroz Blanco (page 66). Top with a squeeze of lime juice.

PESCADO A LA VERACRUZANA

SNAPPER VERACRUZ STYLE

SERVES 4

- 4 red snapper filets
- 2 tbsp vegetable oil
- 2 tbsp chopped garlic (about 7 to 8 cloves)
- 4 red tomatoes, diced (about 4 cups)
- 1 white onion, diced (about 1 cup)
- 2 jalapeño peppers, stems and seeds removed, diced
- 2 bay leaves
- 1 tsp dried oregano
- 3 sprigs fresh thyme
- ¼ cup sliced green olives
- 1 lime, juiced
- Salt and freshly ground black pepper to taste

Preheat the oven to 450°.

Season the fish with salt and black pepper. Place the fish in a roasting pan.

In a large sauté pan over medium heat, add the oil and gently cook the garlic until lightly browned. Add tomatoes, onion, jalapeños, bay leaves, oregano, and thyme. Cook until the onions are translucent, stirring frequently. Add the olives and lime juice. Season with salt.

Add the sauce to the fish and bake for 8 minutes or until the fish is cooked.

Serve with Arroz Blanco (page 66) and Ensalada de Ejotes (page 30).

SALMON CON CALABAZA

BAKED SALMON WITH CALABAZA SQUASH

SERVES 4

- 5 pasilla chiles, stems and seeds removed
- 1 cup orange juice
- 2 tbsp Dijon mustard
- 2 oz piloncillo or dark brown sugar
- 4 8-oz salmon filets
- 4 star anise
- 1 cinnamon stick (6 inches)
- ¼ cup granulated sugar
- ¼ cup red wine vinegar
- 5 cups diced calabaza (3 to 4 lb pumpkin)
- Banana leaves
- 3 tbsp vegetable oil
- Salt and freshly ground black pepper to taste
- Salsa Verde (page 86)

For the salmon:
In a medium sauté pan over medium heat, toast the chiles for 2 minutes or until they start to release their aroma. Remove from the heat. Set aside to cool.

In a blender, purée the chiles, orange juice, mustard, and piloncillo until smooth and the chile is broken down into little pieces.

Place the salmon onto a non-reactive pan or into a ziplock bag. Pour the marinade over the fish, making sure it is completely coated. Refrigerate for 3 hours before cooking.

For the calabaza:
Toast the star anise and the cinnamon stick in a dry pan for 2 to 3 minutes or until they release their aromas. Be careful not to burn them. Remove the spices from the pan. Set aside to cool.

In a medium size saucepan, bring 4 cups of water to a boil. Reduce the heat. Add the toasted spices, sugar, and vinegar. Simmer for 5 minutes. Stir to make sure the sugar is completely dissolved.

Add the diced calabaza to the spiced water, adding more hot water if needed so that the pumpkin is completely covered. Simmer for 5 to 7 minutes or until the calabaza is just tender. (You want the dices to be a bit firm so they hold their shape when reheating.) Remove the calabaza from the liquid and discard the star anise and cinnamon. Set aside to cool.

Preheat the oven to 450°.

(*continued on next page*)

Cut the banana leaves into 4 10"x10" squares. Season the salmon with salt and pepper. Place 1 filet on each banana leaf. Gently wrap the leaves around each of the filets and tie with butcher's string, if needed, to hold them together. Place the bundles in a baking pan. Bake for 8 minutes for medium-temperature fish.

As the salmon is baking, heat the oil in a sauté pan over medium high heat. Add the calabaza. Season with salt and pepper. Cook until golden brown. Add the pepitas.

Serve the salmon filets with the calabaza and Salsa Verde.

CAMARONES AL PASTOR

SHRIMP COOKED WITH ANNATTO AND PINEAPPLE

4 SERVINGS

- 1½ lbs shrimp, peeled, deveined (16 to 20 shrimp)
- 6 guajillo chiles, stems and seeds removed, toasted
- 6 pasilla chiles, stems and seeds removed, toasted
- 1 cup pineapple juice
- ¼ cup red wine vinegar
- 1 small white onion, diced (about 1 cup)
- 1 tbsp achiote paste (annatto paste)
- 1 tbsp dried oregano
- 2 tsp cumin seeds, toasted
- 6 cloves, toasted
- 3 garlic cloves
- 3 tbsps vegetable oil
- 1 small white onion, thinly sliced (about 1 cup)
- ½ pineapple, skin removed, cut in slices, grilled, diced (about 3 cups)
- Salt and freshly ground black pepper to taste
- 4 cups Arroz Rojo (page 67)

For the marinade:
Place the shrimp in a medium size bowl. Season with salt and pepper.

In a blender, purée the guajillo and pasilla chiles, pineapple juice, vinegar, diced onion, achiote, oregano, cumin, cloves, garlic, and salt. Pour the marinade over the shrimp making sure all the shrimp are coated. Marinate in the refrigerator for 2 hours.

For the shrimp:
Heat the oil in a large sauté pan over medium heat. Add the sliced onions. Cook just until the onion is translucent, stirring frequently.

Add the shrimp to the pan. Cook for 1 minute or until the shrimp just starts to turn pink. Turn the shrimp over and cook for 1 to 2 minutes more.

Add the grilled pineapple to the shrimp. Simmer for 2 to 3 minutes, just to blend the flavors. Be careful not to overcook the shrimp.

Serve the shrimp over Arroz Rojo.

LA PUERTA AZUL

MIXIOTE DE BORREGO

STEAMED LAMB SHANK

SERVES 4

- 4 2-lb lamb shanks
- 3 tbsp vegetable oil
- 2 tsp cumin seeds
- 4 cloves
- 1 cinnamon stick
- 4 cups water
- 10 chile guajillos, stems and seeds removed
- 2 tbsp red wine vinegar
- 1 tbsp dried oregano
- 6 garlic cloves
- 4 hoja santa
- 4 avocado leaves
- 4 pieces parchment paper, cut large enough to wrap the shanks
- Salt and freshly ground black pepper to taste
- 2 cups Frijoles Refritos (page 69)
- 2 cups Arroz Blanco (page 66)

In a large sauté pan over medium high heat, add 3 tablespoons of vegetable oil. Season the lamb shanks with salt and pepper. When the oil is hot, sear the lamb shanks on all sides. Do not overcrowd the pan. Work in batches, if necessary. Remove the shanks from the heat. Set aside to cool.

In another pan, toast the cumin, cloves, and cinnamon for 3 minutes. Remove the spices from the pan. Set aside to cool.

In a medium size saucepan, bring the water to a boil. Add the chiles. Reduce to a simmer and cook for 5 minutes. Remove the chiles and reserve the water. Set aside the chiles to cool.

In a food processor, add 1 cup of the reserved water from the chiles, the rehydrated chile pods, vinegar, oregano, garlic, hoja santa, and the avocado leaves. Purée until smooth.

Place the shanks in a non-reactive dish and cover with the purée. Place in the refrigerator and marinate for at least 3 hours.

When ready to cook the shanks, set up a steamer large enough to hold the shanks and a large reservoir of water. Wrap the shanks snugly in the parchment paper. Wrap in foil or sturdy plastic wrap to make sure the juice from the lamb stays inside the paper.

Steam the shanks for 3 hours or until tender. Add boiling water to the steamer, as needed.

Place the shanks on 4 indiviudal plates. Serve with Frijoles Refritos and Arroz Blanco.

FILETE Y PAPAS CON RAJAS

SEARED FILET WITH POTATO AND POBLANO PEPPERS

SERVES 4

- 3 potatoes, peeled, diced in 1" cubes (about 4 cups)
- 4 6-oz beef filets
- 2 tbsp vegetable oil
- 3 tbsp butter
- ½ tbsp chopped garlic (2 to 3 cloves)
- 1 red tomato, diced (about 1 cup)
- 3 fresh thyme sprigs, leaves only, chopped
- 2 cups Rajas de Poblano (page 65), drained
- 2 tbsp crema fresca
- Salt and freshly ground black pepper to taste
- 6 cups Salsa Verde (page 86)

Preheat the oven to 450°.

In a small stockpot over medium heat, add the potatoes. Cover with cold water. Season with salt and bring to a boil. Lower the heat and simmer for 12 minutes or until the potatoes are tender. Be careful not to overcook them. Strain the potatoes. Set aside to cool until needed.

Season the beef filets well with salt and pepper on both sides.

Heat the oil in a sauté pan over medium high heat. Add the seasoned filets to the pan. Sear one side of the filets for about 3 minutes. Turn over. Sear the other side for about 3 minutes. Finish cooking the filets by baking in the oven for 3 more minutes for medium rare.

Melt the butter in a large sauté pan over low heat. Sauté the garlic for 3 to 4 minutes until golden brown. Add the tomatoes and thyme. Cook for 2 minutes or until heated through. Add the potatoes and Rajas de Poblano. Cook for 3 more minutes or until heated through. Gently stir in the crema fresca. Season with salt and black pepper.

Serve on individual plates, Top with Salsa Verde.

COSTILLAS CON EJOTES
BRAISED SHORT RIBS WITH GREEN BEAN SALAD

SERVES 4

- 3 lbs boneless beef short ribs, cut into 3" pieces
- 1 cup Adobo (page 63)
- ½ cup vegetable oil
- 2 medium white onions, chopped
- 3 celery stalks, chopped
- 2 carrots, peeled, chopped
- ½ cup garlic cloves
- 2 cups red wine
- 8 cups chicken broth
- 8 chile de arbol, toasted
- 5 bay leaves
- 8 thyme sprigs
- 1 cup queso fresco
- Salt and pepper to taste
- Ensalada de Ejotes (page 30)
- 2 cups Mole Amarillo (page 91)

Preheat the oven to 325°.

Make sure the meat is completely trim with no silver skin.

Season the short ribs with adobo, salt, and pepper. Set aside.

In a large ovenproof casserole large enough to hold the meat in 1 layer, heat the oil over moderately high heat. Brown the meat on both sides in 2 batches. Transfer to another container. Set aside. Reserve the ovenproof casserole.

Add the onions, celery, carrots, and garlic until golden, stirring constantly. Add the red wine and reduce until almost evaporated. Add the chicken broth and bring to a boil. Add the chiles, bay leaves, and thyme. Bring to a simmer.

Place the ribs in the casserole, pushing down to make sure they are covered with the braising liquid. Cover. Place in the oven.

Bake 2½ to 3 hours, until the meat is tender. Transfer the ribs to individual plates. Serve with Ensalada de Ejotes and Mole Amarillo. Sprinkle with queso fresco.

Note: You can use the braising liquid as a sauce for the ribs by straining the liquid and reducing it on the stovetop until thickened. Pour over the top of the ribs.

POLLO AL LIMON

LEMON CHICKEN

SERVES 4

- 2 lemons
- ¼ cup vegetable oil
- 2 tbsp fresh thyme, leaves only, minced
- 1 tbsp chopped garlic (about 3 cloves)
- 1 3-lb whole chicken
- 1 small white onion, quartered (about 1 cup)
- 2 tbsp butter
- Salt and freshly black pepper to taste

Use a grater to zest the lemons. To avoid bitterness, do not grate the white part of the lemon. Reserve the lemons.

In a small bowl, mix the zest, oil, thyme, and garlic.

Season the chicken with salt and black pepper and place in a roasting pan. Cover the chicken with the zest marinade. Cut the zested lemons in half and insert in the chicken cavity with the onions and butter. Cover with foil. Refrigerate for 1 hour.

Preheat the oven to 450°.

Remove the chicken from the refrigerator and let sit for at least 15 minutes.

Place the foil-covered chicken in the oven and bake for 40 minutes. Remove the foil and continue to cook until an instant-read thermometer inserted in the thickest part of the thigh reads 165°. The drumstick should move freely in its socket and the skin should be a crisp golden brown. Remove from the oven and let rest 10 to 15 minutes before carving.

Serve the chicken with Pipian Verde (page 87) and a bowl of Arroz Blanco (page 66).

LOMO DE CERDO
ROASTED PORK LOIN

SERVES 4

- ½ cup Adobo (page 63)
- ¼ cup vegetable oil
- 3-lb boneless pork loin
- Mole Amarillo (page 91)
- Salsa Pina a la Parilla (page 82)
- Salt to taste

Preheat the oven to 425°.

In a small bowl, mix together the adobo and the oil. Mix well to thoroughly combine, creating a thick paste.

Set the pork loin in a roasting pan. Generously coat the pork on all sides with the adobo mixture. Cover the pan with foil. Let sit for 30 minutes before cooking.

Cook the pork loin for 60 minutes. Remove the foil and cook for another 10 minutes or until brown on the outside and moist in the middle. Check your roast with a meat thermometer for an internal doneness of between 155° and 165°, depending on how well done you like your pork. Remove the pan from the oven. Season the pork loin with salt. Let rest for 10 minutes before slicing.

Serve thin slices of pork with Mole Amarillo and garnish with Salsa Pina a la Parilla.

COMPLEMENTOS

SIDE DISHES

TORTILLAS DE MAIZ
FRESH CORN TORTILLAS

MAKES 24 4"-TORTILLAS OR 14 6"-TORTILLAS

- 3 cups maseca
- 2½ cups warm water

This recipe is for tacos, which are normally made with small tortillas, but you can make the tortillas any size you choose for making enchiladas, chalupas, or larger tacos.

Preheat a comal, cast-iron griddle, or heavy skillet over medium heat.

In the bowl of a stand mixer using the dough hook, thoroughly combine the maseca and water on slow speed. Add the water, ½ cup at a time (you may not need all of the water), until a soft dough forms. Scrape the sides of the bowl, if needed, while mixing. The dough is the right consistency when you squeeze a small portion into a ball and it holds together without being crumbly or breaking around the edges.

Divide the dough into 24 or 14 equal balls. The dough balls should weigh 2 to 4 ounces each, depending on the size of the tortilla you want.

Use a tortilla press and 2 pieces of plastic wrap (a 1-quart freezer ziplock bag split open works best) to make the tortillas. Open the tortilla press and place the plastic wrap or opened plastic bag on the press. Place a dough ball in the center of the plastic. Fold the plastic over the dough ball. Gently lower the top of the press to flatten the dough. Make a 4" or 6" tortilla, about ¼" thick.

Transfer the tortilla from the press to the preheated comal. Cook for about 1 minute on each side. Turn over a third time and cook just until the tortilla puffs up slightly.

Carefully wrap the tortillas in a napkin as soon as they come off the comal or place them in a plastic bag to keep them hot and moist.

ADOBO

DRY ADOBO RUB

MAKES 2 CUPS

- 6 tbsp paprika
- 4 tbsp onion powder
- 4 tbsp garlic powder
- 2 tbsp cayenne pepper
- 4 tbsp ground cumin
- 4 tbsp brown sugar
- 4 tbsp freshly ground black pepper
- 4 tbsp salt

Adobo is a dry seasoning used to marinate meat or poultry. It adds great flavor to your meat and is a wonderful addition to your kitchen pantry.

In a medium bowl, combine all the ingredients until thoroughly mixed. Store in a ziplock bag or a jar with a tight fitting lid.

JALAPEÑOS CURTIDOS
PICKLED JALAPEÑOS

MAKES 4 CUPS

- 2 cups water
- 1 cup white vinegar
- 2 bay leaves
- ¼ cup granulated sugar
- 1 tbsp salt
- 1 tsp dried oregano
- 2 sprigs fresh thyme
- ½ lb jalapeño peppers, stems removed, cut in thin round slices (about 2 cups)
- ½ medium white onion, cut in half, cut again in half length-wise, thinly sliced (about 1 cup)
- 2 garlic cloves, thinly sliced

In a small pan over medium heat, add the water, vinegar, bay leaves, sugar, salt, oregano, and thyme. Simmer for 2 minutes. Remove from the heat and let cool to room temperature.

Combine the jalapeños, onions, and garlic in a jar or plastic container. Add the vinegar/spice mixture and mix gently. Seal and refrigerate for at least 48 hours before serving.

RAJAS DE POBLANO
POBLANO PEPPER STRIPS

MAKES 3 CUPS

- 4 medium poblano peppers
- 1 small white onion, cut in half, thinly sliced (about 1 cup)
- 2 bay leaves
- 1 tsp dried oregano
- 1 cup rice wine vinegar
- Salt to taste

These poblano peppers are great to serve with tacos, quesadillas, or meats. They bring an intense roasted flavor to your table.

Roast poblano peppers over an open flame or grill until the skins are blistered. Turn occasionally to prevent burning. Remove from the heat and place in a bowl. Cover with plastic wrap and let steam for about 10 minutes. When cool, peel off the skins and remove the stems and seeds. Cut into strips.

Combine the pepper strips and the onion, bay leaves, oregano, and vinegar in a bowl. Mix well. Refrigerate for at least 3 hours before serving.

ARROZ BLANCO

WHITE RICE

MAKES 8 CUPS

- 2 cups basmati rice
- 3 tbsp vegetable oil
- ¼ cup diced white onion
- 1 garlic clove, peeled, sliced
- 3½ cups hot water
- ½ jalapeño pepper, stem removed, cut in half length-wise
- 3 cilantro sprigs
- Salt to taste

Place the rice in a fine mesh sieve and rinse under cold running water for 5 minutes. Set aside to drain.

In a large pan over medium heat, add the oil, onion, and garlic. Sauté the onion 5 to 7 minutes or until translucent, stirring frequently.

Add the rice to the onion mixture and cook 3 to 5 minutes or until the rice is opaque, stirring constantly. Pour the hot water into the rice mixture. Season with salt.

Add the jalapeño pepper and the cilantro to the rice and bring to a gentle boil. Reduce the heat to a very low simmer, cover, and cook for 10 minutes or until all the water has been absorbed. Remove the pan from the heat and let sit covered for 5 minutes. Adjust the seasonings, if needed.

Fluff the rice with a fork and serve.

ARROZ ROJO
RED RICE

MAKES 8 CUPS

- 2 cups basmati rice
- 3 tbsp oil
- 1 cup diced white onion
- 1 garlic clove, peeled, thinly sliced
- 2½ cups chicken broth
- 10 oz tomato juice
- 1 red tomato, diced (about 1 cup)
- 3 sprigs cilantro
- Salt and freshly ground black pepper o taste

Place the rice in a fine mesh sieve and rinse under cold running water for 5 minutes. Set aside to drain.

In a large pan over medium heat, add the oil, onion, and garlic. Sauté 5 to 7 minutes or until the onion is translucent, stirring frequently. Add the rice to the onion mixture and cook 3 to 5 minutes or until the rice is opaque, stirring constantly.

Add the chicken broth, tomato juice, diced tomatoes, cilantro, salt, and black pepper to the rice. Stir thoroughly. Bring to a gentle boil. Reduce the heat to a very low simmer, cover, and cook for 10 minutes or until all the water has been absorbed. Remove the pan from the heat and let sit covered for 5 minutes. Adjust the seasonings, if needed.

Fluff the rice with a fork and serve.

FRIJOLES DE OLLA
TRADITIONAL BLACK BEAN SOUP

MAKES 4 CUPS

- 2 cups dried black beans, cleaned of debris, rinsed
- 1 small white onion, diced (about 1 cup)
- 1 sprig epazote
- 1 tsp dried oregano
- 1 bay leaf
- Salt to taste

In a medium size container, cover the beans with water and soak overnight in the refrigerator. Reserve the liquid.

In a medium size stockpot, add the beans, the remaining soaking water, onion, epazote, oregano, bay leaf, and 1 teaspoon of salt. Bring to a boil. Reduce to a simmer and cook until the beans are tender and creamy in the center, about 4 hours. Add boiling water to the stockpot, as needed, so the beans are always covered by at least 1" of water to cook evenly.

FRIJOLES REFRITOS

REFRIED BEANS

MAKES 4 CUPS

- 1 full recipe Frijoles de Olla (page 68)
- 1 cup oil or lard
- 1 small white onion, diced (about 1 cup)
- 3 tbsp chopped garlic (about 10 cloves)
- Salt to taste

Drain the cooked beans. Save the broth to be used to thin the refritos, if needed.

Heat the oil or lard in a sauté pan over medium heat. Add the onion and garlic and sauté until golden brown, about 10 minutes. Add the beans to the pan and mix thoroughly.

With the back of a wooden spoon, smash the beans to make a rustic purée. Add small amounts of the reserved bean broth, if needed, to adjust the consistency.

Season to taste.

GUACAMOLE DE LA CASA

HOUSE GUACAMOLE

MAKES 3 CUPS

- 3 ripe avocados, cut in half, pits removed
- ½ red tomato, diced small
- ½ small white onion, diced small (about ½ cup)
- 1 jalapeño pepper, stem removed, finely chopped
- 2 tbsp chopped cilantro
- 1 lime
- Salt to taste

Scoop the avocados out of their skins. Carefully cut the avocados into cubes and place in a medium size bowl.

Add tomato, onion, jalapeño, and cilantro to the avocado. Squeeze lime juice over the top. Mix well to blend all flavors, continuing to stir until the mixture is a smooth texture. Season with salt.

Serve with tortilla chips.

CARNE A LA PARILLA

GRILLED STEAK FILLING

MAKES 4 CUPS STEAK
1 ½ CUPS MARINADE

- 1 bunch cilantro, heavy bottom stems removed
- 2 garlic cloves, peeled
- 2 sprigs fresh thyme, leaves only
- 2 sprigs fresh rosemary, leaves only
- 1 jalapeño pepper, stem removed
- ¼ cup red wine vinegar
- ½ cup oil
- 2-lb skirt steak
- Salt and pepper to taste

In a blender, purée the cilantro, garlic, thyme leaves, rosemary leaves, jalapeño, and vinegar. With the blender running, slowly add the oil until the purée has a smooth creamy texture. Season with salt and pepper.

Pour the mixture over the skirt steak and let marinate for 3 hours.

Preheat the grill to medium high heat.

For medium-rare doneness, grill the steak on each side for 4 to 5 minutes. Remove from the heat and let rest for 10 minutes before slicing.

POLLO ADOBADO

SPICY CHICKEN TACO FILLING

MAKES 4 CUPS

- 2 guajillo chiles
- 2 pasilla chiles
- 1 tsp cumin seeds
- 1 tsp dried oregano
- 2 garlic cloves
- ¼ cup rice wine vinegar
- 1 cup vegetable oil
- 2-lb chicken breast, butterflied
- Salt and freshly ground black pepper to taste

In a medium sauté pan over medium heat, toast the guajillo and pasilla chiles for 2 minutes or until the chiles start to release their aroma. Remove from the heat and set aside to cool.

Using the same pan over low heat, toast the cumin and oregano for 1 to 2 minutes or until they start to release their aroma. Remove from the heat and set aside to cool.

Remove the stems and seeds from the toasted chiles.

In a blender, purée the chiles, cumin, oregano, garlic, and vinegar together until almost smooth. With the blender running, slowly add the oil until you have a smooth mixture. Season with salt and pepper to taste.

Place the chicken in a non-reactive pan or large ziplock bag. Pour the marinade over the chicken and make sure it is thoroughly coated. Marinate for 2 hours in the refrigerator.

Preheat the grill to medium high heat.

Place the chicken breasts on the grill and season with salt and black pepper. Cook for 3 to 5 minutes on each side or until cooked through.

Note: Another method for cooking the chicken is to mark them on the grill and finish cooking them in an oven preheated to 475°. Cook for 5 to 10 minutes or until cooked through.

SALSAS
SAUCES

SALSA ROJA

RED SAUCE

- 3 medium red tomatoes, cut in half
- 2 jalapeño peppers, stems removed, cut in half
- 1 small red onion, cut in half
- 6 garlic cloves, cut in half
- 2 tbsp vegetable oil
- 3 ancho chiles, stems and seeds removed
- 2 tbsp red wine vinegar
- Salt to taste

Place the tomatoes, jalapeños, and onions on a grill that has been heated to medium heat. Cook the vegetables until they are slightly roasted to develop a nice grilled flavor. Remove from the heat and set aside to cool.

In a sauté pan over medium heat, sauté the garlic in oil until golden brown. Remove the garlic to cool with the grilled vegetables. In the same pan over medium heat, cook the chiles for about 30 seconds on each side or until they turn dark red and release their aroma.

In a food processor, add the grilled vegetables, garlic, and toasted chiles. Purée slowly so the salsa stays chunky. Transfer to a bowl. Stir in the vinegar. Season with salt to taste.

PICO DE GALLO
CHUNKY TOMATO SAUCE

MAKES 4½ CUPS

- 3 tomatoes, seeds removed, diced small
- 1 white onion, diced small (about 1 cup)
- 3 jalapeño peppers, diced small
- ½ cup chopped cilantro
- 2 limes
- Salt to taste

In a medium bowl, combine the tomatoes, onions, jalapeños, and cilantro. Squeeze the lime juice over the top and mix well. Season with salt. Let sit for 10 minutes before serving to allow the flavors to blend.

CHILE DE ARBOL SALSA
ARBOL CHILE SAUCE

MAKES 2½ CUPS

- 6 chiles de arbol
- 2 tbsp vegetable oil
- 3 garlic cloves, peeled, cut in half
- 3 red beefsteak tomatoes, grilled
- 1 tbsp red wine vinegar
- 1 tbsp chopped cilantro
- Salt to taste

Place the chiles in a skillet over medium heat. Toast the chiles for 2 minutes or until they just begin to release their aroma. Turn occasionally to prevent burning. Remove the chiles from the pan. Set aside.

Using the same pan, add the oil and garlic. Cook the garlic for about 3 minutes, careful not to over brown. Remove the garlic and cool to room temperature.

In a blender, purée the toasted chiles, garlic, tomatoes, and vinegar until smooth. Season with salt.

Serve at room temperature. Garnish with cilantro.

CHIPOTLE SALSA
CHIPOTLE SAUCE

MAKES 1½ CUPS

- 3 tbsp vegetable oil
- 1 lb tomatillos, peeled, rinsed, left whole
- ½ small white onion, roughly chopped (about 1 cup)
- 3 garlic cloves, peeled
- 2 chipotle peppers, finely chopped
- Salt to taste

In a sauté pan over medium heat, add the oil and tomatillos. Sauté until the tomatillo skins get blisters and turn a dull green. Turn occasionally to prevent burning. Remove from the pan.

Using the same pan, add the onion and garlic. Sauté until the vegetables are a light golden color. Remove from the heat and cool.

In a food processor, purée the sautéed vegetables until smooth. Transfer to a bowl. Add the chopped chipotle peppers to the puréed vegetables. Stir until thoroughly combined. Season with salt.

If you want a hotter salsa, add more chipotle peppers to taste.

TOMATILLO SALSA
ROASTED TOMATILLO SAUCE

MAKES 2 CUPS

- 1 lb tomatillos, peeled, rinsed, left whole
- 2 tbsp vegetable oil
- 4 jalapeño peppers, stems removed
- 3 garlic cloves, peeled
- ¼ cup rice vinegar
- 1 avocado, peeled, pit removed
- 2 tbsp cilantro, chopped
- 2 limes, juiced
- Salt to taste

In a hot skillet over medium heat, cook the tomatillos until the skins blister and turn a dull green. Remove from the heat.

Add the oil to the same pan and heat over medium heat. Add the jalapeños and garlic. Cook until the jalapeños are blistered and the garlic is golden brown. Remove from the heat and let cool.

In a blender, purée the cooked tomatillos, jalapeños, garlic, vinegar, and avocado until smooth. Transfer to a bowl. Stir in the cilantro and lime juice. Season with salt to taste.

SALSA DE PINA A LA PARILLA

GRILLED PINEAPPLE SAUCE

MAKES 3½ CUPS

- 4 ½"-thick fresh pineapple slices, grilled, diced small (about 2 cups)
- 1 small red bell pepper, diced (about 1 cup)
- 1 jalapeño pepper, stems and seeds removed, diced small
- ½ red onion, diced small (about ½ cup)
- 2 tbsp chopped cilantro
- 2 limes, juiced
- Granulated sugar to taste
- Salt to taste

In a medium bowl, combine the pineapple, bell pepper, jalapeño, onion, cilantro, and lime juice. Season with salt and sugar.

To get a better and more intense flavor from the pineapple, let the salsa sit for 15 minutes before serving. This allows the lime juice to blend well with the rest of the ingredients.

This salsa goes well with pork or fish.

SALSA CRUDA
RAW TOMATILLO SAUCE

MAKES 3 CUPS

- 1 lb tomatillos, peeled, quartered
- 1 white onion, peeled, quartered (about 1 cup)
- 5 jalapeño peppers, stems removed, quartered
- ¼ cup rice wine vinegar
- 2 garlic cloves, peeled
- 1 lime
- ½ cup chopped cilantro
- Salt and freshly ground black pepper to taste

In a food processor, add the tomatillos, onion, jalapeños, vinegar, and garlic. Pulse slowly, making sure the salsa stays chunky. Transfer to a bowl.

Squeeze the lime juice over the salsa and mix well. Add the cilantro. Season with salt and black pepper to taste.

SALSA ROJA
PARA ENCHILADAS

RED ENCHILADA SAUCE

MAKES 6 CUPS

- 10 cups water
- 4 whole red tomatoes, cored (about 2 lbs)
- ½ white onion, quartered
- 3 garlic cloves, cut in half
- 3 guajillo chiles, stems and seeds removed, toasted
- 3 ancho chiles, stems and seeds removed, toasted
- 1 tsp cumin seeds, toasted
- 6 cloves, toasted
- Salt and freshly ground black pepper to taste

In a stockpot over medium high heat, bring the water to a boil. Add the tomatoes, onion, garlic, and chiles. Simmer for 10 minutes or until the tomatoes are tender and the skin is starting to come off.

With a slotted spoon, carefully transfer the simmered vegetables to a blender. Add the cumin and cloves. Purée until smooth. Transfer back to the stockpot and bring to a simmer. Season with salt and pepper to taste.

Reheat the salsa before topping enchiladas.

SALSA VERDE
GREEN SAUCE

MAKES 7 CUPS

- 2 tbsp vegetable oil
- 2 lbs tomatillos, peeled, washed under cold running water, cut in half
- 1 white onion, diced (about 1 cup)
- 2 jalapeño peppers, diced
- 2 poblano peppers, diced
- 6 garlic cloves
- 2 bay leaves
- 2 cups Caldo de Pollo, heated (page 19)
- ¼ cup chopped cilantro
- Salt to taste

Heat the oil in a pan over medium heat. Cook the tomatillos, onions, jalapeños, poblanos, garlic, and bay leaves until the onions are translucent. Add the Caldo de Pollo. Simmer for 8 to 10 minutes. Season with salt. Let cool for 10 to 20 minutes.

In a blender, purée the simmered ingredients until smooth, working in batches, if necessary. Stir in the cilantro. Adjust the seasoning, if needed.

Heat the Salsa Verde before serving. This sauce goes well with enchiladas, poultry, pork, and fish.

PIPIAN VERDE

GREEN PIPIAN SAUCE

- 1 cup pumpkin seeds
- ¼ cup vegetable oil
- 1 lb tomatillos, peeled, washed under cold running water, cut in half
- 1 white onion, diced (about 1 cup)
- 6 garlic cloves
- 6 cloves
- 2 jalapeño peppers, diced
- 2 hoja santa
- 2 epazote sprigs
- 1 bunch cilantro, leaves only
- 3 cups Caldo de Pollo, heated (page 19)
- Salt to taste

In a sauté pan over medium heat, add 2 tablespoons of the oil. Roast the pumpkin seeds for 2 to 3 minutes, stirring frequently. They will release their aroma and start to pop like popcorn when they are toasted. (Be careful not to burn them as they will continue to cook slightly after they have been removed from the heat.) Remove the seeds from the pan and let cool.

After the seeds have cooled, pulse them in a food processor until they are about the size of course grain.

In a medium size saucepan over medium heat, add 2 tablespoons of oil, tomatillos, onion, garlic, cloves, jalapeños, hoja santa, epazote, and cilantro leaves. Cook until the tomatillos are translucent, stirring frequently. Add the Caldo de Pollo and let simmer for at least 10 minutes. Remove from the heat and let cool for 10 to 20 minutes.

In a blender, purée the simmered ingredients until smooth, working in batches, if necessary. Return the sauce to the saucepan over medium heat. Stir in the puréed pumpkin seeds. Simmer for about 5 minutes. Season with salt.

This sauce goes well with poultry, pork, or beef.

MOLE COLORADITO

MAKES 8 CUPS

- 12 ancho chiles, stems and seeds removed
- 4 guajillo chiles, stems and seeds removed
- 1 cup vegetable oil
- ¼ cup sliced almonds
- ¼ cup raisins
- 1 tbsp sesame seeds
- 3 slices white bread, cubed or torn into pieces (about 2 cups)
- 4 tomatoes (about 2 pounds)
- 1 small white onion, quartered (about 1 cup)
- 4 garlic cloves
- 1 tbsp dried oregano
- 1 cinnamon stick, roasted
- 5 cups Caldo de Pollo, heated (page 19)
- 10 oz Mexican chocolate (such as Ibarra), chopped
- Salt to taste

In a skillet over medium heat, toast the chiles for 2 minutes or until they just begin to release their aroma. Turn occasionally to prevent burning. Remove the chiles from the pan and place in a bowl. Soak them for 15 to 20 minutes in at least 4 cups of hot water, making sure they are completely covered.

In a hot skillet, add 2 tablespoons of oil. Fry the almonds until golden brown. Remove the almonds from the pan.

Add the raisins in the same pan and sauté until they puff up. Add an additional tablespoon of oil, if needed. Remove the raisins from the pan.

Continuing to use the same pan, fry the sesame seeds until golden brown. Add 1 more tablespoon of oil, if needed. Transfer the seeds to a paper towel to absorb the excess oil.

Add 2 tablespoons of oil to the skillet. Sauté the bread until golden brown, stirring frequently. Transfer to a paper towel.

In the same pan, roast the tomatoes, onions, and garlic until blistered. Add 1 or 2 tablespoons of oil, if needed.

In a blender, purée the chiles, 2½ cups of hot Caldo de Pollo, and the oregano and cinnamon until smooth. Add additional broth, if needed, to make a smooth sauce. Pour the sauce into a bowl.

In the blender, purée the roasted vegetables, sautéed almonds, raisins, sesame seeds, and bread until smooth adding more broth, if needed, to make a smooth sauce.

(continued on next page)

In a stockpot over medium heat, add 3 tablespoons oil and the puréed chiles. Cook 5 minutes, stirring frequently. Add the vegetable purée and more caldo, if needed. Simmer for 15 minutes.

Stir in the chocolate. Season with salt.

Serve this mole with poultry and white rice.

MOLE AMARILLO

YELLOW MOLE SAUCE

MAKES 6 CUPS

- 8 guajillo chiles, stems and seeds removed
- 3 ancho chiles, stems and seeds removed
- 3 cups Caldo de Pollo, heated (page 19)
- 1 tsp cumin seeds
- 4 cloves
- 2 whole allspice
- ½ lb tomatillos, peeled, washed in cold running water
- 6 garlic cloves
- 3 tomatoes (about 1½ lbs)
- 1 small white onion, chopped (about 1 cup)
- 3 hoja santa
- 3 tbsp vegetable oil
- 1 cup water
- 6 oz maseca
- Salt to taste

In a skillet over medium heat, place the chiles and toast for about 2 minutes or until they just begin to release their aroma. Turn occasionally to prevent burning. Remove the chiles from the pan and transfer to a bowl. Soak the chiles in 2 cups of Caldo de Pollo. Reserve the liquid.

In the skillet used to toast the chiles, toast the cumin, cloves, and allspice for 2 minutes or until aromatic. Using a spice mill, grind the spices. Set aside.

Fill a stockpot halfway with water and bring to a boil. Add the tomatillos, garlic, tomatoes, and onion. Simmer for 10 minutes. Remove all the ingredients from the water. Cool slightly. Remove the skin from the tomatoes.

In a blender, purée the chiles and the Caldo de Pollo they were soaked in. Add more broth, if needed, to create a smooth consistency. Transfer the purée to a bowl.

In the blender, purée the simmered vegetables and hoja santa until smooth. Add more broth, if needed, to create a smooth consistency. Set aside.

In a heavy saucepan over medium heat, add the oil and the reserved chile purée. Simmer for 5 minutes, stirring frequently. Add the reserved puréed vegetables and the ground spices. Season with salt. Simmer for 5 more minutes, stirring frequently.

Mix the water and maseca thoroughly until all lumps are removed. Slowly stir this mixture into the mole until it is the desired thickness.

This mole goes well with beef, pork, or poultry and rice.

POSTRES

DESSERTS

Capirotada

Pastel de Tres Leches

Flan de Vainilla

Flan con Frutas

Churros con Chocolate

Atole

Polvorones y Atole

CAPIROTADA

BREAD PUDDING WITH COFFEE SAUCE

SERVES 6

- 4 cups day-old bread, cut into ½" cubes, dried
- 1 cup walnuts, toasted, roughly chopped
- ¼ cup raisins
- 2 tbsp butter, melted
- 1 cup milk
- ¾ cup granulated sugar
- 3 eggs, beaten
- 1 tbsp vanilla extract
- 1 tbsp ground cinnamon

For the capirotada:
Preheat the oven to 350°.

In a medium size bowl, combine the bread, walnuts, raisins, and butter. Mix well to coat the bread with the melted butter.

In a small mixing bowl, combine the milk, sugar, eggs, vanilla, and cinnamon. Mix well and pour over the bread mixture making sure the bread cubes are well soaked with the egg mixture.

Spoon the bread mixture into 6 4-ounce ramekins. Bake for 30 minutes or until the custard is set and the bread is golden brown and lightly crispy.

Note: This dessert can also be baked in a 9" x 9" baking pan. You may need to increase the baking time by about 10 minutes.

Coffee sauce:
- 1 cup strongly brewed coffee, cooled
- 4 oz piloncillo or brown sugar
- 1 cinnamon stick, toasted
- 2 cups milk
- 2 tbsp dark roast coffee beans
- 6 egg yolks
- ½ cup granulated sugar

In a saucepan over medium heat, combine the coffee, piloncillo, and cinnamon stick. Bring to a simmer and cook until the piloncillo has completely dissolved. Simmer and reduce for 1 minute.

In a medium size saucepan, bring the milk and coffee beans to a gentle boil. Reduce the heat and simmer for 1 minute. Remove from the heat and set aside for at least 20 minutes to better infuse the milk with coffee flavor.

In a medium size mixing bowl, beat the egg yolks and sugar until thoroughly combined. The mixture will look like a thick yellow paste.

Bring the milk back to a simmer. To temper the egg mixture, carefully ladle a small portion of the hot milk into the eggs, stirring constantly to keep the eggs from cooking. Continue to add small portions of the hot milk mixture to the eggs, stirring with each addition, until the egg mixture has come up in temperature. Add the egg mixture back to the pan of the remaining hot milk.

Remove the cinnamon stick from the coffee mixture. Pour the coffee mixture into the egg/milk mixture. Simmer over medium heat for about 5 minutes, stirring occasionally.

Strain the sauce through a fine mesh strainer into a small heat-proof container. Let cool, stirring occasionally. Cover and store in the refrigerator until ready to use.

To serve, remove the capirotadas from the ramekins and place on dessert plates. Drizzle with a generous portion of the coffee sauce.

PASTEL DE TRES LECHES

THREE MILK CAKE

SERVES 6

Sponge cake:
- 1 cup pastry flour
- 1 tsp baking powder
- ½ cup milk
- 14 oz sweetened condensed milk
- 12 oz evaporated milk
- 4 eggs, yolks and egg whites separated
- ¾ cup granulated sugar

Three-milk syrup:
- 1½ cups milk
- ¼ cup dark rum
- 14 oz sweetened condensed milk
- 12 oz evaporated milk
- 1 tbsp vanilla extract

Garnishes:
- 2 cups whipped cream
- 1 cup raspberries
- Mint leaves

Preheat the oven to 350°. Lightly butter 6 ramekins and dust with all-purpose flour.

In a medium bowl, sift the flour and baking powder together. In another medium bowl, combine the 3 milks and whisk gently to make sure they are well combined.

In a stand mixer, beat the egg whites until they are light and foamy. With the mixer on low speed, slowly add the sugar. Add the egg yolks one at a time, making sure they are well incorporated after each addition before adding the next yolk. Add 1/3 of the milk mixture to the egg mixture and combine. Add 1/3 of the flour to the egg mixture and combine. Continue to add the milk and flour alternately until each addition is mixed evenly, ending with the flour.

Evenly divide the batter between the 6 prepared ramekins. Bake for 30 minutes or until the center of each little cake springs back from the gentle touch of a finger. Place them on a cooling rack to cool.

To assemble the cakes:
In a medium bowl, combine all of the milk syrup ingredients (milk through vanilla extract). Stir until well mixed.

(continued on next page)

When the sponge cake is completely cooled, pierce the cakes 5 or 6 times with the tines of a fork. Slowly spoon the syrup mixture over the cakes, allowing time for the syrup to saturate the cakes before each addition. Make sure the cakes are completely soaked with the syrup. (There will be extra syrup left over for garnishing.) Cover the cakes with plastic wrap and refrigerate for at least 1 hour before serving.

To serve, carefully ease the cakes out of each ramekin onto individual dessert plates. Drizzle with extra syrup. Top with a spoonful of whipped cream, a raspberry, and a mint leaf.

Note: This cake can also be baked in a 9" x 9" baking pan. You may need to increase the baking time by about 10 minutes.

FLAN DE VAINILLA

VANILLA FLAN

SERVES 6

- ¾ cup granulated sugar
- 1½ cups heavy cream
- 1½ cups milk
- ½ vanilla bean
- 3 eggs
- 4 egg yolks
- ½ cup granulated sugar for caramel

Preheat the oven to 325°.

For the caramel:
In a small pan over low heat, add ½ cup sugar. Stir occasionally until the sugar melts into a caramel and turns a medium golden color. Pour the caramel into baking ramekins, making sure to coat the bottom of the ramekins and up the sides. Set aside.

For the custard:
Combine the cream and milk in a saucepan. Scrape the seeds from the vanilla bean into the cream mixture. Bring the cream to a simmer over medium heat. Remove the pan from the heat and let steep for 10 minutes.

In a bowl, whisk the eggs, eggs yolks, and sugar until they are well blended. Slowly add the cream mixture into the egg mixture without creating a lot of foam.

Pour the custard into the ramekins. Set the ramekins in a water bath, cover, and cook for 40 minutes until gently set. Chill overnight.

FLAN CON FRUTAS

FLAN WITH FRUIT SALAD

SERVES 6

There are various versions of flans in Mexico, this is one of them. We make this flan when we celebrate something special like a Holy Day, birthday, or Christmas.

This flan is usually served with fresh fruit to cut down on the flan's richness.

- ½ cup granulated sugar
- 3 eggs
- 14 oz sweetened condensed milk
- 14 oz evaporated milk
- 1 tbsp vanilla extract

For the flan:
Preheat the oven to 350°. Set up a water bath with a baking pan filled with 1" of water.

In a small pan over low heat, add the sugar. Stir occasionally until the sugar melts into a caramel and turns a medium golden color. Very carefully, pour the caramel into 6 baking ramekins, making sure to coat the bottom of the ramekins and up the sides. Set aside.

In a medium bowl, beat the eggs. Add the condensed milk, evaporated milk, and the vanilla extract. Whisk slowly until well mixed.

Pour the milk mixture into the ramekins and place them in the prepared baking pan. Cover the pan with aluminum foil. Bake for 45 minutes or until a knife inserted in the center of a flan comes out clean. Remove and let cool.

Fruit salad:
- 1 cup blue berries
- 1 cup raspberries
- 1 cup sliced strawberries
- 1 tbsp minced mint
- 1 tbsp granulated sugar
- 1 lime
- 3 tbsp confectioner's powdered sugar for garnish
- 6 mint leaves

Wash the berries and dry on paper towels. In a medium bowl, combine the berries, mint, sugar, and a squeeze of lime juice. Mix gently.

Prepare the fruit garnish at least 10 minutes before serving for better flavor. Top the flans with fruit garnish, a berry, and a mint leaf.

CHURROS CON CHOCOLATE

FRITTERS WITH CHOCOLATE SAUCE

- ½ cup granulated sugar
- 2 tsp ground cinnamon
- 2 eggs
- 2 cups water
- 2 oz diced butter
- ½ tsp salt
- ½ cup granulated sugar
- 1 tbsp baking powder
- 1 cup pastry flour
- Vegetable oil for frying

On a shallow plate, combine sugar and cinnamon, making sure it is evenly mixed. Set aside.

In a small bowl, beat the eggs. Set aside.

In a medium size saucepan over medium heat, combine water, butter, and salt. Bring to a full boil to melt the butter, stirring to make sure the salt is dissolved and everything is well mixed.

In a stand mixer, slowly mix the flour and baking powder on low speed, adding the water until a firm dough forms. Add the eggs. Mix until they are fully incorporated into the dough.

Place the dough in a bowl. Wrap in plastic wrap and refrigerate until thoroughly chilled.

In a medium size saucepan or deep fryer, add enough oil for a depth of at least 2". Bring the temperature up to 350°. Line a large plate or baking sheet with paper towels.

Fill the chilled dough into a pastry bag fitted with a ½" (No. 7) star tip. Carefully squeeze the dough into the heated oil, making 5"-long churros. Fry for 2 to 3 minutes on each side, using tongs to turn them. Transfer the churros to the paper towels to drain the excess oil.

Dust the hot churros with the sugar/cinnamon mixture.

Chocolate sauce:
- 2 cups semi-sweet chocolate chips
- 1½ cups heavy cream

In a medium size saucepan over medium heat, bring the heavy cream to a simmer. Add the chocolate chips, stirring constantly, until the chocolate melts into a smooth sauce.

ATOLE
HOT CINAMMON MILK

SERVES 6

- 6 cups milk
- 4 oz piloncillo or brown sugar
- 2 cinnamon sticks, toasted
- ¼ cup water
- 2 tbsp maseca

In a medium size saucepan, bring the milk, piloncillo, and cinnamon sticks to a gentle boil. Reduce the heat and simmer for 5 minutes or until the piloncillo is completely dissolved.

In a cup, mix the water and maseca to make a smooth paste. Add this to the simmering milk and stir with a whisk. Simmer for 5 minutes and serve hot.

Note: To make champurrado, finely chop one tablet of good Mexican chocolate and add to the simmering milk mixture.

Atole

Atole is a traditional hot drink in Mexico that is prepared with corn masa to thicken the milk. It is often prepared with a chocolate called champurrado.

Atole is prepared on special occasions, Holy Days, or Christmas Day and is also an accompaniment for churros.

POLVORONES Y ATOLE

SUGAR COOKIES AND ATOLE

- 1 cup butter at room temperature
- ½ cup confectioner's sugar
- 4 tbsp milk
- 1 tsp vanilla extract
- 2 cups all-purpose flour
- 1 tsp baking powder
- ½ cup walnuts, roasted, chopped

Garnishes:
- 1 cup confectioner's sugar
- 1 tbsp ground cinnamon

Preheat the oven to 325°.

In the bowl of a stand mixer, beat the butter, confectioner's sugar, milk, and vanilla extract at medium speed, scraping the sides of the bowl as needed. Add the flour and baking powder slowly, scraping the sides of the bowl to make sure it is mixed evenly. Mix until it is a soft, smooth dough. Gently fold the walnuts into the dough.

Using a tablespoon, make small balls of dough and place them on a baking sheet about 4" apart. Using your thumb, flatten the balls into a round shape. Bake the cookies for 20 minutes or until lightly browned around the edges.

Arrange the cookies on a platter. Sprinkle with powdered sugar and cinnamon.

BEBIDAS

DRINKS

Margarita Classica

Margarita con Granada

Azul Martini

El Diablito

Tijuana Speedball

Tequila

Tequila is well-known all over the world for its unique taste and bouquet. It also mixes well with other ingredients when preparing cocktails—margaritas being the most famous.

The production of tequila began over 200 years ago in the town of Tequila in Jalisco, Mexico from where the name and all production came.

Tequila is liquor distilled from the fermented juices of the heart of blue agave, also known as maguey. Blue agave is a bluish green plant with long, sharp, pointy leaves and a large heart, which is what they use to extract the pulp and distilled tequila.

There are dozens of brands of tequila and they are divided into five different categories:

- Oro (gold): Un-aged, young, and adulterated, which means there is caramel coloring and oak extract added so that it resembles aged tequila

- Blanco or silver (white or silver): un-aged

- Reposado (rested): aged a minimum of two months but less than one year in oak barrels

- Anejo (aged or vintage): aged a minimum of one year but less than five years in oak barrels

- Maduro or extra anejo (extra aged): the newest additions to the tequilas and aged a minimum of three years in oak barrels

The aging process changes the color of tequila, but tequila is also colored with caramel to make it look darker.

Anejo is darker, reposado a little lighter, and blanco or silver has no color at all. That is how you can sometimes tell the difference between tequilas.

MARGARITA CLASSICA

CLASSIC MARGARITA

1 SERVING

- 2 oz Jose Cuervo Gold
- 1 oz Triple Sec
- 1 oz freshly squeezed lime juice
- Salt (optional)
- Lime wedges for garnish

To prepare the glass with salt, run a wedge of lime around the rim of the glass. Gently dip the damp rim in salt. Margaritas can be served without the salt rim, but a salted rim is the classic way to present this drink.

In a cocktail shaker, place 9 ice cubes. Add all the ingredients and shake vigorously for a few seconds. Pour into the prepared glass.

Garnish the glass with a lime wedge.

MARGARITA CON GRANADA
POMEGRANATE MARGARITA

1 SERVING

- 2½ oz tequila reposado
- 2 oz pomegranate juice
- 1 oz Cointreau
- ½ oz fresh lime juice
- Salt (optional)
- Lime wedges for garnish

Prepare the glass with or without salt as directed in the Margarita Classica recipe.

In a cocktail shaker, place 8 or 9 ice cubes. Add the rest of the ingredients and shake vigorously for a few seconds. Pour into the prepared glass. Add the ice cubes and stir gently.

Garnish the glass with a lime wedge.

AZUL MARTINI
BLUE MARTINI

1 SERVING

- 2½ oz Malibu rum
- 2 oz Blue Curacao
- 2 oz pineapple juice
- ½ oz lime juice
- ½ oz Sprite
- Maraschino cherry or orange peel for garnish

Place all the ingredients in a cocktail shaker. Add 9 ice cubes and shake vigorously for a few seconds. Pour into a martini glass, straining the ice as you pour it.

Garnish the martini with a maraschino cherry or orange peel.

EL DIABLITO
THE LITTLE DEVIL

1 SERVING

- 2 oz tequila blanco
- ½ oz cassis liquor
- ½ oz fresh lime juice
- 2 oz ginger ale
- Lime wedge for garnish

In a 12-ounce glass, add 10 ice cubes and all the ingredients accept the lime wedge. Stir gently with a straw.

Garnish the glass with a lime wedge.

TIJUANA SPEEDBALL

- 1 shot espresso coffee
- 1 oz Herradura reposado
- 1 oz Kahlua
- 1 oz Baileys
- Espresso beans for garnish

Combine all the ingredients in a cocktail shaker. Shake vigorously for a few seconds and pour into a martini glass.

Garnish with espresso beans.

Ingredients

Chiles
(dry and fresh peppers)

Ancho chile (wide chile) is the dried form of poblano peppers; anchos are dark, flexible, and mild with a semi-sweet taste.

Chipotle is ripened and smoked dried jalapeño, rehydrated in water before using or it can be ground to make chipotle powder. It can be very hot. They are used to make sauces, soups, and salsas.

Chile de arbol (tree chile) does not come from a tree. They are long thin pods that come from a tall plant. The pods are green when fresh or bright red when dry. They are used mainly in salsas and can be very hot.

Guajillo is orange-red in color. They are very popular in Mexico and have a sharp flavor. Medium hot, they are used in sauces, adobos, and broths.

Jalapeño (the name comes from Jalapa, Veracruz) is the most common of all chiles. They are medium hot and used mostly in raw form in salsas. They can also be pickled or stuffed with cheese as they are in chile rellenos.

Morita are small, dark, and brightly colored. They are also known as mora. Some people use them as chipotles. This chile is a variety of jalapeño and has a smoky flavor.

Mulato is brownish-black and wrinkled when it is dried flat. (Not to be confused with ancho.) Mulato has a chocolate-tobacco flavor and is used in moles and stews.

Pasilla are pods that are large and narrow with black skin. They are a mild pepper, very rich in flavor, and used in sauces and moles.

Poblano (the name comes from puebla) is dark green and mild with a fruity flavor. It is used to make rajas, chiles rellenos, and sauces.

How to Toast Chiles

Many recipes call for toasted chiles. The best and easiest way to toast chiles is on a hot skillet or griddle, roasting both sides until they release their aroma, but making sure not to burn them.

To rehydrate chiles, you can soak them in salted water. This also reduces come of their spiciness.

Herbs and Vegetables
(dry and fresh)

Achiote (annatto) is the seed of an inedible fruit that is harvested solely for it seeds. It can be used as a condiment to color food such as cheese, recados, or adobos in Mexican cooking. Achiote can be found as a paste or as dry seeds in most stores.

Hoja de laurel (bay leaf) is a fragrant, dark green leaf when it's fresh or olive green when dry. It is used in stocks, soups, and sauces.

Calabaza, also known as West Indian pumpkin, is a squash with a firm texture and sweet flavor, very similar to butternut squash. It has a hard skin that is yellow or green. Sizes vary from jicama to watermelon size. It is baked or roasted so that the pulp can be scooped out because it's difficult to peel.

Cilantro (coriander) is typically chopped raw in salsas, antojitos, and to flavor broths and soups when it is cooked.

Chayote comes from Mexico and Central America. It's a small vegetable in the squash family and is the size of a pear. It's light green, with smooth skin, and white in the middle. Chayote can also be found with prickles on them. It's used in salads, stews, and soups in Mexico.

Epazote is a long, green serrated leaf with a strong flavor. It's used to cook beans, soups, broths, and fish. Epazote is not eaten raw because of its strong flavor and slight bitterness. It's also used for medicinal purposes as a tea to remedy stomach discomfort.

Jicama is a legume that looks like a large potato or radish. When peeled, it has a crunchy flavor and can be eaten raw. Jicama does not have a lot of flavor but contains a high percentage of vitamin C. It's used in summer salads and special diets.

Hoja santa (holy leaf) is an aromatic herb with a strong flavor similar to anise. It is bright green and heart shaped when fresh. It's used in southern Mexico to wrap tamales the same way you use a banana leaf or corn husk. Hola santa is also used to cook fish and make green sauces and moles.

Hoja de aguacate (avocado leaf) looks like a large bay leaf and is olive green when dry. It has a licorice flavor and is used in mixiotes, barbacoas, soups, and sauces.

Hoja de platano (banana leaf) is a dark green tropical leaf that is long and wide. It's used to wrap tamales and barbacoa.

Nopales are a green vegetable also known as cactus pads, the young stems of the cactus pear plant. Very rich in vitamins A and C, they have spines, a tart flavor, and a crisp texture.

Oregano is of two types—Greek or Mexican. Mexican oregano has a more intense flavor and is less sweet. It blends well with chiles and the cumin flavors that are used in Mexican cooking. Oregano is mostly used in sauces and moles.

Cheeses and Dairy

Chihuahua is a soft dairy cheese made from cow's milk and used primarily for melting, for example, in quesadillas. It is named after the state of Chihuahua in the north of Mexico.

Cotija cheese is a sharp goat cheese similar to parmesan. It is used in salads, bean soup, and various antojitos.

Crema fresca is crème fraîche that is used primarily for garnishes and dishes such as tostadas, enchiladas, rice, and sauces. Crema fresca does not separate when cooking with it.

Queso fresco is a spongy white cheese that is typically a combination of cow and goat milk. It is a little acidic and grainy and is used in antojitos, tostadas, and enchiladas.

Queso Oaxaca, also known as quesillo o asadero, is originally from the state of Oaxaca and is made with cow's milk. This cheese is hand stretched into long ribbons and has a tangy, creamy texture. It is similar to mozzarella and is used in quesadillas.

Others

Comal is a cooking utensil, a cast iron plate used to cook tortillas, quesadillas, grilled steak and other dishes, and can also be used to blister chiles.

Maseca is corn flour made from ground dried corn. It is used to make tortillas, bocoles, and picadas and is used in many Mexican dishes.

Piloncillo is the name given in Mexico to small blocks of unrefined cane sugar. Piloncillo usually needs to be grated or melted before being used in sauces and dessert.

GRACIAS POR ACOMPAÑARNOS

LA PUERTA AZUL RESTAURANT

2510 Route 44

Salt Point, NY 12578

(845) 677-AZUL (2985)

www.lapuertaazul.com